LAST CALL

Also by Stephen Kessler

POETRY
Garage Elegies 2018
Where Was I? 2015
Scratch Pegasus 2013
Burning Daylight 2007
Tell It to the Rabbis 2001
After Modigliani 2000
Living Expenses 1980
Beauty Fatigue 1978
Thirteen Ways of Deranging an Angel 1977
Poem to Walt Disney 1976
Nostalgia of the Fortuneteller 1975

TRANSLATION
Forbidden Pleasures (poems by Luis Cernuda) 2015
Poems of Consummation (poems by Vicente Aleixandre) 2013
Desolation of the Chimera (poems by Luis Cernuda) 2009
Eyeseas (poems by Raymond Queneau, translated with Daniela Hurezanu) 2008
Written in Water (prose poems by Luis Cernuda) 2004
Aphorisms (prose by César Vallejo) 2002
Heights of Machu Picchu (poem by Pablo Neruda) 2001
Ode to Typography (poem by Pablo Neruda) 1998
Save Twilight (poems by Julio Cortázar) 1997, 2016
From Beirut (poem by Mahmoud Darwish) 1992
Akrílica (poems by Juan Felipe Herrera, translated with Sesshu Foster) 1989
The Funhouse (novel by Fernando Alegría) 1986
Changing Centuries (poems by Fernando Alegría) 1985
Widows (novel by Ariel Dorfman) 1983
Homage to Neruda (poems by eight Chilean poets) 1978
Destruction or Love (poems by Vicente Aleixandre) 1976

FICTION
The Mental Traveler (novel) 2009

NONFICTION
Need I Say More?: Portraits, Confessions, Reflections (essays) 2015
The Tolstoy of the Zulus: On Culture, Arts & Letters (essays) 2011
Moving Targets: On Poets, Poetry & Translation (essays) 2008

EDITOR
The Sonnets by Jorge Luis Borges 2010

LAST CALL

STEPHEN KESSLER

BLACK WIDOW PRESS
Boston

Black Widow Press is an imprint of Commonwealth Books, Inc., Boston, MA. Distributed to the trade by NBN (National Book Network) throughout North America, Canada, and the U.K. All Black Widow Press books are printed on acid-free paper, and glued into bindings. Black Widow Press and its logo are registered trademarks of Commonwealth Books, Inc.

Joseph S. Phillips and Susan J. Wood, Ph.D., Publishers
www.blackwidowpress.com

Acknowledgments

"How to Look" first appeared in *Catamaran.* "Jalapeño Poem" first appeared in *Chicago Quarterly Review.* "So Long William" first appeared in *New American Writing.* "Emily's List," "Sweeping the Courtyard," "Balcony Poem," and "Inscribed on a Marble Slab" first appeared in *Osiris.* "Gray Eminence" first appeared in *Red Wheelbarrow.* The author extends his gratitude to the editors of these magazines.

"North Beach Night" first appeared in the anthology *Fog and Light: San Francisco through the Eyes of the Poets Who Live Here* (Blue Light Press).

Thanks also to Irene Bablé Marruffi of Cádiz, Spain, for permission to publish her group of poems "Confinamiento" and the translation "Lockdown."

The author also wishes to thank these esteemed readers for their friendship and encouragement: Walter Martin, Kay Bradner, Carolyn Tipton, Leslie Tremaine, Barry Fruchter, Marc Hofstadter, Doreen Stock, Kate Todd, Roger Greenwald, Joseph Matthews, Christina Waters, Frank Galuszka, Zach Buck, Joel Leivick, Mark Primack, Maggie Paul, and Gary Young.

Cover photo: No Title (hand on lips), 1928 © Man Ray 2015 Trust / ADAGP – ARS – 2021, image : Telimage, Paris
Author photo: Joel Leivick
Cover design and book production: Kerrie Kemperman

ISBN-13: 978-1-7371603-0-4

Printed in the United States
10 9 8 7 6 5 4 3 2 1

for Claire & Alex,
Lita and Felix

Contents

PANDEMIC CADENZA

LAST CALL

I endure the sensitivity of my feelings with an attitude of disdain.
I have all the qualities for which romantic poets are admired,
and even the lack of those qualities,
which makes one a true romantic poet.

FERNANDO PESSOA
(trans. Richard Zenith)

The Muses won't repulse in grey old age
The man on whom they smiled when he was young.

CALLIMACHUS
(trans. Walter Martin)

OVERTURE

After the Plague

The sight of you alive
with no screen between
is something worth trying not to die for

but who are we now
and would we know each other
after this long exile

protected by these antiseptic
hazmat suits
these hand-sanitized plastic gloves

these plexiglass shields
these protocols of the tested
and the disinfected

for a while we were mostly human
but that was in another century
since then we have sacrificed

to survive the reign of terror
of the microbes
and the clueless rulers

deprived of funerals
we grieve from an unsafe distance
where what we've lost feels farther away

even than the absence
of your presence
you I saw for the last time

one time long ago
when our next embrace
our next meal

was guaranteed by our existence
by our appetite
for intimate understanding

now it's not so clear
I'm not so sure
so much has occurred

even remembering is beyond reason

BAD LUCK CHARMS

Epilogue at Seventy

Fate arrives to twist you out of shape,
stripping away the mate and a place to sleep,
the home whose walls held the art of your ever after,
what felt like a kind of contentment—
uneasy, somewhat restless, marbled with longing yet rich in its way—
and leave you in disorienting rooms, better than under a bridge,
tabula rasa galleries, high ceilings and acoustics of echoing independence
with strings attached, an orphan enchanted princess left in your loco
    parentis.
It is, the resident monk assures you, a philosophical opportunity,
yet the crypto-erotic entanglement with every other woman you know
or ever knew complicates meditation, you can't shake the sticky kisses
left by every last one, all and each of those escaped shoulderblades
who bequeathed nothing but a lingering smell of her skin
and the afterimage of a serenely radiant face.
Bereft, helplessly remembering, blended into their legends
as surely as they are into yours, mixed inextricably
in unwritten history, shifty in its illusory and elusive slippery
intimacy, you reach for that fetching form and find it missing,
what smiled for a flash and vanished
to leave a dead-of-winter night and a cold drizzle, edge of a storm
forecast to hit hard in the hard hours, days, decades ahead
when seas will be higher than even washed-up Melville imagined,
spilling their tears all over town like torch singers.
And so your doom isn't yours alone,
singled out as you are, but is rather a common catastrophe
of a magnitude so immense as to be immeasurable.

Destiny's Gravity

When the wind at your back
is a cold draft and you're going no place,
you're lucky to be wearing an Italian scarf, all wool,
to keep your pencil neck from a bad chill,
which will stiffen with time until the mirror tells you
it is too late and you must make do with what you've done
and with what has been done to you, complex twists
of fate you didn't see coming and they caught you anyway
and the current carries you and you swim or think
you are swimming or keeping your head
above water when all around losers are blaming you
for their losses and you confess you can't be sure,
it seemed clear but now you don't know,
some things change, people you could swear
were there disappear and you begin again
to grasp destiny's gravity.

Gray Eminence

My t-shirt today is gray, my shirt is gray,
my beard is gray, I am a gray man in a gray mood
though the sky is blue and the flowers at the farmers market
are yellow and the lips of some of the Saturday girls are red
and the fiddle-and-mandolin music is bright
as a summer morning in the mountains.
I was up there once and remember its green smell
and the sweet blue-black stains on fingertips that had picked
wild berries on a trail along the creek. But
I have been shrinking,
incredibly, inexorably, to fit a more urban flat
on Death Row, where my reduced footprint will go
unnoticed because of my advanced youth.
I don't seem bereft, I had my fun and did what I could
to help, but the headlines tell me it's all over, and I can't help
wondering if I made a bad turn somewhere,
took this out-of-the-way road to my dream
and lived it largely awake and woke up
to nothing much but these sheets of lost
beds with loves in them and pages of poems
I always got mixed up with those mates,
I could hardly tell them apart until it was too late.
Now I write them letters in my sleep
confessing everything but they don't reply,
that gate is shut, garden gone wild, no way back.
This must explain my eminence above all,
so far removed I have gone gray,
cloudlike in my darkening lightness.

Who Could've Said

Who could've said, back when
it began, that it would end
like this, in the Presidential Suite
of a century-old hotel with no
bellhop in sight, no crime
of passion or otherwise,
just the subtle hum of Highway 1
near midnight on Halloween,
diminished day of the dead,
haunted grandfather on a shelf
with scars from trying to drive
his truck across the streetcar tracks
wrongly timed—he was drunk—
his rich son framed
on the kitchen counter
grinning with cigar in his box
at the track, in a picture
snapped by his wife's lover,
and his son in turn
with pen in search of what
could spill or tell or spell
or spit the whole tale
in cascading lines
like one of those toys
shaped like a loose spring
that walked itself downstairs
in the fifties—a Slinky—
or the ball you could turn
over and it told your fortune
but not really, it couldn't have foretold
what a winning hand

you'd be dealt nor how you would lose
so much and have so much
to show for it after all,
words nobody believes
but you know what they mean,
how much they count
what's gone that remains,
what is grieved and gives back
its vague and vivid taste
on a tongue with nothing left,
dripping with kisses
that could not be kept
but flowed elsewhere
leaving only this.

Bad Luck Charms

I throw my hat on the bed
I walk under ladders
I pet black cats that cross my path
I step on cracks
I leave the house and go back in without turning around and spitting
three times
I smash mirrors
I spill salt without throwing it over my shoulder
I step twice in the wrong rivers
I brag about things I haven't done
I fall in love with women who don't reciprocate
I fall in love with women who reciprocate
I fall in love with women who fall for others
I lend money to friends I never see again
I drive on the wrong side of the road
I put my pants on backward
I drop out of school
I volunteer and don't show up and quit
I get disinherited
I get hemorrhoids
I'm going bald
I can't find a place to park
I scrape my fenders in parking structures
I catch colds
I miss flights
I'm accident prone
I forget to bathe
I don't take my meds
I don't make my bed
I wear the same socks three days in a row
I tempt fate

I don't celebrate holidays
I don't pet dogs
I listen to the news
I click on links
I talk to robots on the phone
I run out of ink
I get up on the wrong side of the bed
I put my shoes on the wrong feet
I walk with a smirk
I work for less than minimum wage
I age without grace
I don't remember why
I don't know how
I lose my way
I made some bad turns
I thought my luck would change
and I was right

Widowers

Dean of the arts whose beauty queen bride
after fifty years wed had a bad end, drawn out too long,
now he's alone in their dream house
with a huge view nobody hardly sees.
Avant poet whose twin muse match went out
one night in her sleep, just like that,
like a light gone dark,
nobody home, no tears goodbye, last words,
rhymes in tongues,
and now he's moved so far from their nest
her spirit has to stretch a continent across
to whisper savory nothings into his listenings.
"Sparkling, no ice?" says the sweet voice
of the flight waitress handing a plastic cup
as requested by the translator bereft
of his linguist wife who left him
for an illness past understanding, beyond
repair, perpetual spiral vortex
into negative space,
a darkness no one can fathom
least of all the one left.
He cups his hands
around what light he can.

Recurrent Date

This must be the anniversary of something
first coupling of a couple since split up
date of some natural disaster
        catastrophic in its displacements
deadline of assignment long overdue
all my aced papers archived
        in the museum
                or mausoleum of star students
so many honors mounted on the wall
like heads of x-loves in a Fellini film
speaking again those murmured
        moans and groans
siren songs of long-gone consummations
you knew it was too late even then
and that made it all the more
        what it was for a few minutes
coming around again
like clockwork and still catching you
        shocked to swim twice in the same
                time
such dark hours these
shortly before midnight
when night hangs not quite tired
        in the sleepy eyes
shy of the same dream that recurs
her just out of reach
not home when you get there
rode off with a new love
and nothing you can do

Lost Books

Every time I hear the title of one
I remember I had a copy once
that now is lost,
loaned to a friend and never seen again,
left in some room in some city
or on some road, a motel
or hotel room, some lover's room
I couldn't leave soon enough
because the sex was wrong,
half a library left behind when I moved,
a book traded or sold because I thought
I'd never need it again
or had never read it and figured I wouldn't
but now I miss it, influenced
by its absence. Books
too numerous to remember,
read and unread, books in boxes
lost in the mail in a long move,
in breakups, left in the pockets
of airplane seatbacks, in backseats of taxis,
on toilet tanks, on subway trains,
books I must have been born to lose,
books written by friends,
by me, an embarrassment
of misplaced, misbegotten,
misunderstood, badly skimmed or flipped through
mostly paperback but also clothbound
books. I might have wanted
to reread one,
and now—
nothing on the night stand

(I don't read in bed)
where that book should be.
Beds are for sleeping
and mating, not reading
except for all those women I knew
who read in bed.
I have abandoned, neglected,
left splayed face down
or face up spread wide open,
spine cracked,
more books than I can account for,
ones I'd be better off
reading now
than doing this—but
what can you do,
they looked good on the shelves
in one house, one apartment
or another
and now are gone.
Mourned too late, they escape me
like runaway cats
I couldn't catch,
bound griefs
I forgot to memorize
because I know by heart.

Kessler Syndrome

> The Kessler syndrome ... is a scenario in which the density of objects in low earth orbit is high enough that collisions between objects could cause a cascade where each collision generates space debris that increases the likelihood of further collisions. One implication is that the distribution of debris could render space activities and the use of satellites in specific orbital ranges infeasible for many generations. —*Wikipedia*

Instead of attending the Apocalypse Festival,
millions of emergency last meals of vanishing civilizations
served to long lines of dazed refugees strangely savoring
every moment before it's all over,
the unmoved monk stays home and meditates
emptily while the world whirls through his skull like a brainstorm,
brilliant idea gone bad and spun into nothing, flying debris
and piles of ruined possessions which by their moldy wreckage
prove their pointlessness. Sirens of first responders
wail and warble above the combustive hum
of weekend cars on Route 1, everyone trying to escape,
which is why the acolyte is hunkered down,
comfortably ensconced in the Sacred Bunker
across from Holy Cross Church and the Zen Center.
He is unaffiliated, unfit for human company
and thus unaccompanied even by a cat
much less the mate of his dreams who left him long since
for stranger embraces. Wounded gravely, still alive enough
to delight in a smile delivered brightly across a counter,
he allows that pleasure too to pass through and prove him
porous, holier than most in his riddled condition.
The thorns of life had no velocity,
they guarded cultivated beauty in some English garden,
but the projectiles slicing the wild sky are unidentified
flying junk, not romantic at all, and they can kill.

Nothing to be done but relish the rhythm
of the roofers' hammers across the street
proceeding as if shelter were still possible.

Increasingly Posthumous Poem

Increasingly posthumous, after the fact,
ready for the coda, the obit, the backward glance
down Highway 1, you will never travel that road again
through all the old losses, your shotgun companions
navigating other journeys equally unbelievable,
now you know what you never could have imagined
as you sped through those handsome landscapes
whose trees flickeringly graced you with transient summer light
turned strangely autumnal in its oddly inspiring slant,
that angle signaling a fresh start after all the evidence,
when you can almost see something more to be done,
as if in preparation for the unexpected, one last good turn,
one final face to savor in its radiance,
reminding you again of what you miss.
Ah, nothing illuminates like the new dark—
it tries to close your eyes but you can't stop looking
at such dangerous beauty destined to take your last breath
with its final blessing.

Speedy and Preppy

Speedy and preppy, the boy in the black sports car
is suddenly half a century older and slower
in the darkness of the auditorium where he is entertained
by the audience in advance of the stars onstage.
He has earned anonymity hiding behind a byline
and appearing in public as Joe Normal,
the guy he aspired to be in high school,
and how perennial to observe the same drama as ever,
even the same name called but addressed to another
in the voice of a dear friend's
dear friend, how intimate is that—
no escaping the closeness
of the overlaps, time in a tightening
or widening spiral that comes around always again
and again in recurring circles until you are dizzy
with coincidence and synchronicity,
links galore in the Great Chain of Fools,
of which you are a superb specimen as proved
by your unstoppable stupidity, opening your heart
and your lips to so many to no avail. And so the roller
flows with the blackened blues in the same ways
through all the long years and long drives home alone.

Out of It and Over the Hill

It's a relief to be irrelevant,
invisible to the days' stars,
a relic of lost time whose scars
can be felt only by sensitive fingers
whose absent touch is gone for good
and in its place gazes that don't engage,
distracted and absorbed, consumed
by screens shrunk to a size no matinee
idol would recognize. Once you were as
beautiful as that, heads spun
when you entered a room,
and now almost nothing's left of that
magnetism, you're a fly on the wall
witnessing with all eyes on the lookout
for the swatter so you don't wind up
splat and that's that. That's what's
coming soon enough but there's too much
to do, nothing as it seems, it is
what isn't until you make it so, so you must
surprise yourself if no one else
with what otherwise wouldn't be.
Your assignment is to stay alive
long enough to see, to witness
what you can't, mustn't miss,
what passes without a trace if you don't
catch it long enough to contemplate
the way it mirrors, reflects certain essences
you recognize but can't quite describe.
Above and beyond, unimpeachably undeniable,
viable in what afterlife is left.

Dry Warmth on a Drizzly Night

The floor is littered with bad drafts, wrong starts, false
moves that get you shot in old movies but in real life
no one is the wiser because nobody's looking,
they're listening
for intimate whispers lost with those long winds
and limbs of long lost time echoing unintelligible
sounds once gasped when nothing could say
what it was the uttering mouth felt, so close
it could be touched but just out of reach too,
elusive as anything ever glimpsed, like that very face,
possessed. Whose was that, you wonder—surely not hers
who no longer hardly exists, so long in the tooth you are both
over the hill with longing for that long gone peak
stripmined for what memory can be scraped.
Even that much glows
a little, though, gives enough dry warmth on a drizzly night
to light the pillow or page enough to write on the faint gray lines.
Lose something in translocution from the ecstatic,
the grief-stricken?
Can you even read that music?

Unemployed Conductor

Stripped of my players
disgraced for having made them
too much mine
trying to transmit the soul
of music moving through us
our bodies the instruments
of ecstatic edification
melodies that transcend understanding
I'm left with my baton alone
and no podium no tails no starch
in my shirt and no adoring eyes
responding virtuosic to every move
of my expressive hands
at least those nights
in the high-toned hall whose acoustics
held us in our warmest sounds
passed more than once through us
blessing us
now what's left
of our consummate accomplishment
is an echo a faint resonance
of sonic memory
museumlike in my abandoned galleries
but I can't retire
the scores are too strong too unsettled
the charts too exquisite in their
hieroglyphic eloquence
they must be played by someone
even me in exile

What Didn't I Know

What didn't I know that couldn't become more
unknowable in its investigation,
how to interrogate its witnesses
who weren't sure what they had seen
or where it went in the next blink,
there was no trail, scarcely a trace
of what transpired so obviously
anyone could explain if they had known
to notice, but the moment
got away and by the time it mattered
it was long gone, and now there was nothing
to be done but try to leave room
for its return, when it would speak
for itself and say what had made
no sense at the time but now
meant more than anyone
could be sure—it was a mystery,
truly, with no private eye
to figure it out, which is why
I had to try myself, but it was no use.

BENEFACTORS

Reading Ferlinghetti near Midnight in His 99th Year

We are all shrinking
we aging bards
our spines
compressing
with the weight
of gravity
but the old man grows
the oldest man alive
the youngest of the ancients
is growing still
his stature increasingly
statuesque
as he survives the terrible weathers
lashing the sad planet
weathers the changing climes
with his steady light
paints light
lifts the light lines
of his timely
rhymes
his casual mastery of white
page space
which only a shadow would presume
to impersonate
bald head blue eyes blue jeans white beard
easy courage gleams
from the shy glance
modestly proud
of his self-made monument
his monumental
accomplishment

his anarcho-capitalist business model
three historic stories
of "trees made immortal"
painterly writing
on walls whose brilliant windows
above the traffic
flash through fog
like the last lighthouse
what wit it would take
to match with his
what stamina to keep up
with his workouts
what words what silences what typography
to trace the arc
of his trajectory
waves of wandering homage
ripples of raw awe
nibble at his cliffs
how has he done this
no one knows
but he has
and he goes on
shining through time

Emily's List

Emily D. was a bad influence
on me, she put me on her list
and kept sending me poetical
appeals, cryptic quatrains

that rang in my head like hymns,
like little prayers with squeaky rhymes
or back-of-the-envelope calculations
adding up to a sum I didn't understand.

Those notes are more or less the sum
of their heroics, I mean hieroglyphics
without spell check or special effects,
casting a spell analogous to existing

acoustics, old folk songs strummed
on gleaming guitars in dark halls
where idolatrous devices in idle hands
cast odd light on oddly enchanted faces.

Mine is not one as I am only
on Emily's speed dial, hotline
from her lines to mine with
no medium in sight, just a subtle

philosophical hum of long unknowing,
ambiguous and paradoxical, sound of Emily's
sweet nothings intimately whispered
in tongues when we were young.

Letter to Bukowski

Dude, you've been dead
for more than two decades
and you keep on publishing new poems—
how do you do that? Oh yeah,
I saw the files at Black Sparrow
in Santa Rosa when I was living up on the coast
recovering from massive heartbreak,
and because your voice on dark nights made me laugh
and your letters always took me seriously,
I drove in one day to see your partner Martin
and he showed me the long drawers where he'd stashed your poems
to bring out later, in your afterlife.
On a gray day in Surf City
passing through Logos I found a stack
of one of those books, remaindered after seven printings,
one of your lesser sellers.
You make it look so easy
and you make it new
in a way old Ez would've hated maybe,
but like Sinatra you did it the only way
you couldn't help doing it, the only way you could.
You, as few others in this sorry business,
are good company still, wherever your ashes blew,
wherever you are,
whatever dive bar or desk
you're sitting at
still typing and drinking,
drinking and
typing.

So Long William

You were always elusive
allergic to emulation
articulating the ineffable
your language liquid
quicksilver slippery
to trace the unsayable

gone overnight
as if lifted away
on winglike eyebrows
a little wickedness
or mischief in your grin
you've slipped out of sight

no way to describe
or explain your gravity
underground power
soft as a whisper
intimations of intimacy
in the gliding lines

speeding along the freeway
south of San Francisco
you passed me a joint
you'd pulled from your pocket
with a bemused expression
as if surprised

I'm losing the way
wrongly unraveling
ruining what could've been

a song in your honor
wanting to prolong
your presence in your absence

the elite type of your Olympia
the handsome scribble of your hand
your work gloves that fit mine
in France that time
years after you'd left
your garden neglected

you won't be held
no spell will arrest you
nor rescue you
who have spared yourself
by saving what escaped you
leaving us to wonder

—for WSM

Old White Men

Poe and Nietzsche beckon from the used-book bin,
recent arrivals just in from the 19th century, far enough gone
to be forever up to date for one perennial retrospectator
longing more acutely than ever for the past's
presence, for what has lasted.
Would I have liked to know those guys
or were they more difficult
than the distressed everywhere now, on edge
with dread and bad health and dreadful ideas
that drive them over the edge, so overwrought
by what passes for history
hijacked by psychopaths
they've lost their minds.
Mine seems to be still here, still searching
for something to read that will make sense,
will please and intrigue with enduring insight
absent now from all these arguments.

Borges's Belt

This sash
was wrapped
around the
Obra poética
New Edition,
Revised and
Corrected,
a book
whose pages
are delicious
to the touch
and blissful
to read
slowly,
one poem
at a time,
and from which
to translate
lovingly,
every line
of every
sonnet
spoken
on paper
in a new
tongue,
rhymes
turned around
or upside
down or inside
out to refine

and reflect,
to echo
their sounds
in a way
so persuasive
as to deceive
the reader's
ear and delight
the eye
with parallel
shapes
on the white
page,
the whole
volume
spilling its
music
into fresh
arrangements
that flow
with the tone
and the mood
and the formal
dignity
of the original
even though
the form
is only
a facsimile
and the sound
cannot replicate
but only
imitate

the Castilian
in an English
tinged with
American and
vaguely British
accents
because Keats
was Georgie's
first hint
at the melodic
meaning
of poetry.
I take this sash
for a belt
and type
these lines
in a vain hope
of holding up
my baggy jeans
for which
I have grown
too bony
in my old age
for the cut
of the waist
to hold them up
on my skinny
butt, where
words
are all I have
to rest my
case on, to
declare my

dedication,
to make anything
of anymore as I
meet gravitas
half way, holding
up my half
of the deal
I made when I
pledged allegiance
to the same
muses
as he.

Guide Dogs

Homer had one,
name of Argos,
whom he loaned to Odysseus
for his homecoming.
Milton had his, who
answered to Adam,
a wretched cur who lost his bitch
to a sneaky snake.
Joyce called his dog
Freud, who peed in streams
of consciousness the scribe
tried to catch in a glass jar
from which he would take
dictation. Borges,
a Georgie-come-lately
lost in labyrinths
of his own construction
with nary a spare string
to find his way out,
enlisted one, Ariadne,
and her sibling Aleph,
expert sniffers
of first things, roots
and routes. Me, I am
a cat person, mainly
into sleeping, curled
on a comfy chair,
unconcerned, unleashed,
a little shy
of time and slightly
inclined to rhyme,

purring at a cool pace
to give the dogs
pause. All those pooches
knew their masters' ways
and ghosted some of their
best lines, but my cat
is not like that,
couldn't recall who he licked
last night much less
what they whispered,
which he did not transcribe.
If you need a guide,
don't count on Fellini,
he's busy doing nothing
for me, but Watson,
IBM's robodog, is it; it
is the only dog
that doesn't shit.

How to Look

It's been explained already, always and forever,
those rainbows in the oil puddle,
cloud herds migrating after a storm
in puffy accumulations across the sky,
tough leaves sprouting from cracks
in a rock wall—all ordinary
as anything and equally mesmerizing
when framed in a glance or a gaze—
those eyes easily even more amazing,
all you need do is see
what's there, wildly controlled
as sirens attuned to an emergency.
Those long lost lives caught in a click
and frozen in a photograph
in a book that fetches from a city street
a disorienting image
ephemeral in its fleeting uniqueness
stopped once in a river
you never stepped into
except those countless times
along all those sidewalks you ever strode
in search of what? Eyes
that might see you back, return
your transient glance? And how
do you look to them? Too cool?
Too curious? Too omnivorous
for everything your hunger meets
as your eyes eat everything in sight?
All of the above
and below also
and in the periphery as well,

wraparound vision even a camera
can't quite catch,
but in your imagination you have seen it all,
you know it all in all the false leads
you followed, all the true
loves you lost, the words
you tried to hold them with
through which they slipped,
elusive as light itself
illuminating everything
you ever saw.
Look again. It is all still there
and gone.

—after Garry Winogrand

"Trust Your Own Voice"

Sage advice from one not of this world
whose path I crossed by chance
by happenstance
one of so many I can't count
but an all-star team
of all-time greats
whose names are known
and whose friend I was
even briefly
in some way
some harmonic connection
for a few seconds
or days or years or decades
like Duncan who said
Trust your own voice
what a dazzling madman
genius poet scholar
who came into the seminar
and said everything
at once in no discernible order
but somehow it made sense
and hung together and left you
thinking
about poetry

Epigrammatical

Walter, your Martial artistry
runneth over-the-top, spilling its light
and weighty pleasures into my lap
with Latin-lover wit and suavest gravitas.
Its fine-tuned, sharp-honed lines
that make me laugh and groan
with clean obscenity
and low sublimity
are timelessly antique, like you,
miles above and beyond
the clueless currents, the no-place-fast
traffickings of the careered,
the overworkshopped, the academonic,
the kakaphonic. Melodiously idling
like a big rig parked for coffee
at a Texas truck stop
towering above the pedestrian pickups,
your subtle rumblings resonate
over the heads and taillights heading home
on all the interstates
that lead to Rome.

—homage to the classical knockoffs of Walter Martin

Googling the Greek Anthology

On libraryofbabel.net
you click on Ancient Greece and there you are,
hanging with Anonymous and all those other oldtimers
still horny as hell and taking eternal revenge
on their x-girlfriends,
narrating with unreliable wit
their jealousies and fantasies,
obscenities, pornographies, involuntary
celibacies and spurts of accidental gratification.
Epigrammatical because who has time, their zingers
sting the singers while those slippery gals
escape into afterlives of their own
where they don't give a kiss who's dissing them
as long as their names are spelled
immortally and trans-texted accurately and snappily
in Texas English with rhymes in the right places
set down by some old autodidact
timewarped after the fact
but just in time.
Their too-late barbs are balm for bad dreams
kept at bay in the deep hours
when sleeping would mean missing,
all alone, those silent partners
inscribed in stone.

—for WLM

Haiku Book Review

Dan Barth's book—
unlike most poetry,
it's fun to read

Master haikuista—
to be expected,
lives near Ukiah

Gabbing too long,
he's late for dinner—
old poets talking

Wisdom and Vigor
turning a double play
at second base

Bukowski tells a joke
to Gary Snyder—
Gary laughs out loud

Buddhist and Taoist
walk into a bar,
go with the flow

Effing true to life
no effing way—
ineffable truths

California English,
not Japanese—
who's counting syllables?

Home in Kentucky,
sweet family stories—
luck of the draw

Poems written by
a man in a good mood—
almost unheard of

Still building fires
with wood he cuts himself,
bringing real warmth

Horses on the track,
rumbling music of hooves,
poets in the saddle

Silks flash in the sun,
hot dog with lots of mustard
on a fresh bun

Having too much fun
makes writing a poem seem
easier than it is

Real poems, real poet
publishing in the margins
for a happy few

Memo to JFH

We are so different, dude,
you agitating for collective love,
improvising optimism out of atrocity
with rabbinical aplomb and the congregation
following in the echoes of your baton,
me ever more existential, solo, negotiating
the long curves turning inward
in exploration of conditions
only the comfortable can afford to contemplate.
But I dig your shtick,
your Whitmanic Ginsbergian Nerudist generosity,
expansive beyond your own inner circles,
leading journeys into territories
no paper can contain—
even fame can't tame you,
no identity enough to fix your filibuster,
you just keep on
as I continue too
in my own multitude-containing caravan
across the succulent wildlands
so colorful in their solitary subtlety
the vigilantes mistake me for a native.
You on the other hand are unmistakable,
identifiably unbreakable
and inspirational,
uncontainable in your neverending overflow.
That's why this much later
I hear you from here.

—for Juan Felipe Herrera

Reading Leonard Cohen

I'm reading Leonard Cohen
he sounds better on the page
than other ways I've known him
on a record or a stage

a sucker for desire
he plunged into the flames
which I more or less admire
cause he wasn't playing games

wounded in the wars of love
he couldn't help but wage
he struggled to make wisdom of
an unholy horny sage

his songs are one-note monotones
redundant in their sound
his images like rolling stones
that barely skim the ground

he makes it look so easy
he makes it look so hard
he tries to make it breezy
but his soul is scarred

I don't know what I'm saying
nor do I know why
writing is like praying
to an empty sky

the old monk was a Buddhist
the old goat was a Jew
we met when we were nudists
down in Malibu

we bodysurfed together
on different sets of waves
in different kinds of weather
with different babes

we weren't exactly brothers
but we knew each other well
and had each other covered
as far as we could tell

he got pretty famous
I stayed more obscure
no muse could ever tame us
and we sure couldn't tame her

so here's to Leonard Roshi
and here's to Rabbi Cohen
whose prayers were hardly kosher
but they could pass for poems

Another Memo to Z.

You keep returning to libraries
for something to do for a living,
it's honest work, even noble
in its book love and understanding
of its own nobility, humble
as pushing a cart and slipping volumes onto shelves,
helping patrons find what they want,
what they need,
as you need books, but you keep
getting fired, you can't take orders,
you favor the sweet disorders
of association, imagination, improvisation,
not the best fit for an institution,
but you keep coming back
because books are the best
companions, better than people,
you can take them to bed and they expect nothing
and meet you half way
in sympathetic recognition
like the faces of certain women
you don't know
in passing and to whom you don't speak
so the mystery lingers,
and so you return to the stacks,
to the information desk, to the shelter
of what you can trust
despite the bosses' badnesses
because you can take it
or leave it
and you keep doing both because

you like it, this cycle of life
and death, of coming and going
and getting paid
for doing nothing
more than hanging out with books,
your dream job, a career
worth quitting,
worth keeping.

Bolaño on the Beach

He's scribbling something in the sand with a stick
he stole or found washed up like an old poet
who he used to consider canonical but now
their work is scarcely worth ransacking
for a phrase, an anecdote, an image or two
to spin into his own image because
he's shameless, this Bolaño, who can't stop writing
even as high tide will wipe it out,
is driven to read and recount unendingly
everything that ever happened or was written
and revered or reviled in his pantheon
of manic paragons and depressive poseurs
who nevertheless represented something
worth writing down, around, above and beyond
or about, Bolaño turns it all to his own
recombinant mumbo-jumbo because he's helpless
to defend his genius against himself,
he's scribbling in the sand because he can't stop
inscribing his stream or steam or scream
of consciousness on every surface in sight
until his world, his endangered habitat
is swarming, writhing with words or worms
that escaped the can and now can't be caught
or put back, they're too slimy
and slippery to be fixed in print
and that's why the beach is the best medium
and why he's wearing shades and smoking
a Spanish cigarette whose black tobacco
is inspiring and stimulating and killing him
and he's happy because he's being consumed by the sun.

James Dean Crossing

On State Route 46
between US 101 and Interstate 5
Route 41 north jogs
        between Shandon and Cholame
and the driver must take a left
with no traffic light
against traffic coming west along 46.

One day in September 1955
Jimmy Dean in his silver Spyder
        low slung to the road
its color blending with the gray pavement
was speeding west toward the road races
                at Pismo Beach
        or was it Pebble Beach
or possibly Torrey Pines

and Mr. Turnipseed in his pickup truck
                cruising east on 46
        and turning north onto 41
failed to see the low-flying roadster
        which hit his truck head-on
killing the coolest driver of the coolest car
those roads have ever known.

Today traversing the same route from LA
because the 101 was covered with mud in Montecito
from the rockslides that followed the wildfires
        that stripped the hillsides
driving that route round trip for the first time
on my way home from a poetry reading

I sped past the site of the fateful crash
marked by a simple sign
James Dean Memorial Crossing—

flying along with the flow averaging over 80
just a couple of CHP cruisers seen all day
and sesame rice crackers and a tangerine to sustain me
I blew by in my Subaru
          silver gray
with little dents and scratches in the corners
from thousands of miles negotiating turns
          in parking structures—
pause button for a bumper sticker—

and made it safely home in record time.

Photo of My Mother circa 1968

I found it in a drawer after her death,
a business card size shot,
Nina reclining in a white ensemble
on the slope of a sand dune on Point Dume,
curve of the Malibu coast and cliffs
over her shoulder, hair flipping in the breeze,
big smile on her face
for the photographer, her lover,
though she was still married to my dad—
it was the sixties
and she was in her fifties
and still good looking with her good looks
and all the cosmetic help she could afford,
and Jack had lost interest
and she still desired
and needed the adoration,
so Solle with his camera
was her camera man—
and here she is in this picture,
fifty years later in a little frame,
on a shelf with her father's pocket watch,
which has no hands,
looking happy and sort of sexy
and politely wild
leaning like that with her sleeve
pressed into the patchy land
and her bare feet
in the sand,
the old print bleached out,

faded with age, with time, an image
disappearing into a haze
of forgiving and obliterating light.

Photo of My Father in 1925

Standing hands in pockets
of a fine wool double-breasted
beige overcoat,
hat cocked at a casual angle,
necktie, dark slacks, well-shined shoes
on a Seattle sidewalk
in front of Hirsch-Weiss showroom
where he was working,
he looks mature and serious
yet kind and friendly,
relaxed expression,
calm focus in his eyes
at seventeen, maybe sixteen,
just a kid but already a senior
in the streets' prep school,
Green's Cigar Store,
where the touts and hustlers hung out,
and now he was on his way
in sportswear sales, an entrepreneur
in the making—it would be years
before his blind date with my mom
and then three kids
and the move to LA
and then me, and then success and wealth
until his death at Cedars-Sinai in '83—
he's young in the picture, seasoned
having missed a frivolous adolescence
thanks to his dad's desertion,
he grew up fast and proud
of how grounded he is,
how well dressed,

how well held in a moment
slowly fading into a sepia haze
of unrecoverable recollection.

Fat Jack at the Track

In his box at the wire,
in his blue plaid sportjacket,
big eyeglasses shining, big
cigar in his hand, an open program
unfolded on the rail alongside binoculars,
my father is grinning
in his favored habitat,

touts coming by with tips
and gossip from beyond the backstretch,
characters, he called them,
storytellers and first-class horseshitters
with colorful histories
in the streets and hangouts
where the big boys yakked and placed their bets.

The picture was shot by the ex-vaudevillian
who'd taken his place
in my mother's bed
by the time he sent it to me,
in a frame, no less,
a memento of their day at Hollywood Park.

Maybe Bukowski was in the stands that afternoon,
maybe on the way back to their cars—
Jack's Cadillac in valet parking,
Buk's VW bug out on the lot—
they took a few parallel strides, crossed paths
before returning to their respective worlds
and understandings of chance,
the long-shot bet,

unpredictable payoff,
last two dollars lost.

Between the ringing of the starting gate
and the thunderous rumble of the photo finish
happiness flashes,
and between races
they celebrate their luck,
relishing the brief relief.

My Cat Pessoa

In my old age
I'm going to adopt one last cat
and call him Pessoa
a cat with glasses
reserved
purring in several languages
rough tongue licking
remnants of sauce from the pasta bowl
Here Pessoa
I'll call at mealtime
and he'll come trotting
his tail a question mark
curious
green eyes gleaming
warming my lap at winter solstice
cooling my mood as the globe roasts
Pessoa you're such a dignified
companion
graced with detachment
and something like compassion
as you keep me
humbler than I'd be otherwise
aloof but kind
my role model
nimble graceful light on your feet
with sensitive whiskers
tough equanimity
and irony
good old Pessoa
my silent partner
in anonymity

GHOST BARS OF CALIFORNIA

Gray City Song

Would that my hair
were that white
walking on Hayes
Street with my
sweetie on a Sunday
afternoon instead
of just dull gray
sipping a cocktail
at Hayes Street Grill
inside looking out
at the gray city
slanted with spring
sun at 6pm, but
this is good, gray
as I am, the Grey
Goose gimlet slightly
sweet but dry enough
to satisfy my need
to see what's in
front of me, lovely
pedestrians of every
elegant kind wrapped
against the chill breeze
and grays of April
buildings rinsed almost
clean by rain, chaser of
city water to cleanse
its suffering gray
sidewalks.

Gallows Music

Italian red on the brass bar
in the pizzeria of your choice
is all you have left after the last crisis,
the bride absconding at the last minute
with her backup man, a Dracula lookalike
with a silver stake to drive through your heart
with the sledgehammer he carries on a rack
in his Hummer, perfect vehicle for rocky getaways
with a mattress in back for romantic emergencies.
Left at the gallows, you imagine a whiskey glass
with a scoop of gelato to cool your throat
after your screams have died down and you are
hugging the hangman for cold comfort.
He was about to officiate at your consummation
when the bride fled and the whole weight of the dirty trick
destiny played landed on your head like a lead crown
you thought was laurels in the dark distance,
closer than it looked at the time and now
on top of you like a ton of Sunday papers,
more bad news than you know what to do with
despite your credentials, your battered ID
flashed at crime scenes, disasters, wars and domestic
tragedies, wives out of control, husbands
who couldn't help themselves, who snapped
and slammed out the door before they did something
irreparable. Noir is the color of their true loves' lips
which lash them again and again and they never learn.
Gelato soothes but that is not enough.
You must keep sipping the darkness until you are drunk

with impotence, powerless unless some spell may be said,
some jujitsu move to flip fate using its own dead weight
against it and as it sails over your head you hear a song.

Having a Beer in Fort Bragg

I went to pray for her but the church was locked
and the brewery across the street was open
so here I am sipping a Pilsner at the far end of the bar
under the football game, but I can see baseball at the other end.
It's Saturday afternoon and two hours to showtime
at the bookshop, one more vain effort to reach a reader,
anyone with whom the words might resonate, echo
unspoken thoughts or unearth
unspeakable feelings, unimagined impressions
but all true, in the way everything is
troublingly true.
So we are here, customarily unaccompanied
when almost everyone else is coupled up,
greasy fingered with fried things
delicately shoved between lips
before the kissing begins. You are beyond this
even while here, "It's like I'm here
but I'm not here," as the busgirl puts it
near the end of her shift, shuffling mugs
and crashing plates into tubs to be sent back
to the dishwashers.
The slender glass of golden suds
is too slim even to sip slowly
before it's gone, but to get drunk
at this hour is in bad taste
and dangerous with all the driving
you have to do. So you must nurse
what little is left
and make it last.

North Beach Night

Neon buzz above Columbus on Columbus Day
is night's way of reminding us we are not Indigenous
people trying to sleep in the Hotel Bohème but interlopers,

incredulous that beatniks have become respectable,
their portraits on bathroom walls like those of bankers
and industrialists in uptown Midwest steakhouses.

City Lights shines through the midnight haze
of fires razing the state and darkening patriarchs
taking over the globe with their towering hotels,

so unlike here where the doors use steel keys
and the stairs bear stains of shoes
that have trudged these streets in search of poetry.

Listening to Yuja Wang Play Beethoven at the Santa Cruz Civic

Steinway & Sons is stamped in gold leaf on the black piano,
which I can see from row J on the center aisle,
        seat bought tonight at the ticket window,
my luck to land a wheelchair spot nobody wanted,
I can even see the orange streaks in the pianist's hair
to match her sexy dress,
        can ogle her naked legs,
                her feet in black stiletto pumps
keeping the beat with a light touch on the pedals.

The folding chairs on the basketball court are hard,
but not as bad as the steeply raked stands
        where you're lucky to get down the steps
                without pitching head first into the orchestra.

Yet we are here feeling the strings' vibes rippling through our flesh
and our ears surprised by the sweet soulfulness of the German,
        a word that still sends shivers through me,
                in his deafening bliss, his search
for the right syncopation
        in the delicate solo
                played by Chinese fingers
I wonder what Ludwig would think about,
        those bare arms in eveningwear
as if to seduce the music with their brainy shape,
coaxing sounds out of the instrument that echo
        off the open lid,
which blocks my view of the conductor's back,
        jumping this way and that with his baton
and bush of long hair bouncing, gesticulating

to get the most out of the orchestra,
which hits those notes
with high heart, accurate to the task.

But what would the composer make of this building,
a roller derby venue not a concert hall,
where the architecture and the music don't mix
but the sound transcends,
reaches beyond the roof,
beyond the sirens of the engines
from the fire station next door
moaning and wailing
into the twilight of a summer night.

Old Man with a Horn

What would you do
without these horns
of the young dudes
on stage blowing,
bending their rage
through brassy reedy
wiry machines of
sound screaming
through twilight
ink on the fading
page, pen picked up
at the Business
Expo, Insight
Education, for just
such occasions as
this listening,
recording, tran-
scribing and trans-
lating what can't
be said but must
be sung anyway
because the old
man is horny and
must do something
with what fire he
has, so blow, geezer,
blow, be boldly old
and unstopped by
time, still unbelieving
your eyes at your luck
in still being, still

seeing the young
coming alive in
these timeless age-
less forms, these
bodies channeling
spirits uncrushed
by news, what the
rulers are doing,
unnatural disasters,
ruses of the power
flashers, music the
juice of rejuvenation
even for those
too over the hill to
look up from their
notebooks long enough
to lament their
fate but go on
blowing coolly into
the dark blue light.

Ghost Bars of California

Juliette Binoche, Ruth Bader Ginsburg and Pope Francis
are in town, I saw them at the Nickelodeon
and after the movie they adjourned, like me,
a few minutes later, to Oswald, cool restaurant
named after a presidential assassin,
where a man drinking a martini
had started a conversation with me
just before they entered
and took seats at the other end of the bar.
A couple of stools to my right, I heard
"How's it going?"
He caught me while I was musing
on the good looks of the staff.
"Talking to me?"
He was, and he needed to talk,
and the bartender was busy with the new customers,
white robed, black robed, and sexily disheveled in Parisian nonchalance,
so he told me about his family's ranch in Hollister
and how he had made and lost two fortunes in business,
and showed me on his smartphone some of his photographs
from a book he was working on,
Ghost Barns of California,
and that he'd grown up around great wine
because one of his grandfathers was a vintner
and he loved to humiliate sommeliers
by asking them a trick question about the wine
because he couldn't tolerate pretentiousness
and that his grandmother'd been an English professor
at Stanford, and knew six languages.
He ordered another martini
and told the bartender to bring me another beer

whether I'd drink it or not, I could look
at it, and he kept talking.
I was distracted and kept glancing over at the celebrities,
as if the bartenders and waitresses weren't attractive enough,
but the man's monologue was interesting,
he was giving himself a pep talk to try some new thing
at fifty-three, his black-and-white photo book
or some startup something-or-other
that would get him through middle age in the style he liked.
He said he used to write poetry but decided it was self-indulgent.
I agreed completely, but then no more so
than telling your life story to a stranger over drinks.
I finished the second Pilsner and wished him well,
we'd probably meet again at this marble slab,
but when I turned,
La Binoche, RBG and the pope
had paid their tab and gone.

Old Ponytails

Are all these balding geezers with gray ponytails
the same hippies I took acid with at Altamont?

They look like those guys only so much older
I wouldn't recognize their lives or their old ladies,

or mine for that matter, foretold by some Gypsy
soothsayer yet still not easily believed, so long in the tooth

I can hardly chew this Cuban cigar I tote
in my shoulder holster like a pacifier

that fails to fill in for the missing nipples.
I sip my own spit, I nibble at the savory shape,

but I lack a match, can't feel in my lips
its full effect, its fatal flavor released.

Whatever all these old men know I could say too
if I had the hair, but my crown is cropped

and the trimmed laurels are in the soup
and except for the beret I'm playing it straight.

At Gabriella Café

Keeping the cooks up late,
the last man out alone
on a slow night
gets in the gate
before the kitchen closes,
is indulged, orders a glass of red,
a salad, a bowl of pasta,
and has the house to himself
except for a lingering
couple on a blind date,
or late-life lovers,
or married forever,
but together on the last Tuesday
in time at nine o'clock,
music down the block
too loud by half,
just African enough
for white folks wiggling in back,
so the last man sitting
steps out for a stroll
and has landed where no one
is waiting, but a kind woman
brings him wine.

—for Paul Cocking

Pieces of LA

End of an endless day
on a road that never ends
but runs from one end
of your odyssey to its
beginning and back
again where only you
are small enough to see
incredibly shrunken to a child-
size facsimile of your lost
self in some funhouse
where your family
once dwelled and you
alone are all that's left
of the evidence.

::

No newspaper to be had anywhere,
everyone has a screen and who needs news
anyway, it's bad, bad men rubbing women the wrong way,
dictators doing what they will, refugees on the run
with no place to shower or shit—
these grievous lines will mark you for life
indelibly as they are inescapable
and will track you past all the whistling graveyards
and ash-scattered friends you tried to sing back
into existence, all the solo meals
in out-of-the-way cafés
where something you couldn't say
tried to break the ice,
all the faces you serenaded to no avail

because they weren't available,
or to your astonishment they swooned
into your bemused embrace
and what good did it do,
a flash of sweet relief
followed by long trails of tears
running in rivulets through the refugee camps.

::

Was it your heart or head that needed shrinking,
having swelled helplessly against its own better health—
it had to, didn't it, you don't know why.
Nor do the weather women know what to make
of the deserts drifting through the cities,
bookstores dried up and blown down dusty roads
where pilgrims hauling print detectors
scan for something to read
or sit in their vehicles idling in traffic
until the lights change, and still they sit,
cool DJs in faraway studios trying to soothe
with moody grooves of the up-and-coming
studs and sirens of the waves,
some comfort, it's true, but the fumes
seep through almost like inspiration
and spell their spells on the walls of puzzled skulls.
How long a wait until the healer will see you
and cast some counter-incantation
to cast out the demons of your dismay?
It seems like decades you've been sitting here
scratching the same questions
into whatever surface made itself felt.

::

Now you are downtown discovering a city
driven but also built and fallen apart
and partly rebuilt with all the sounds
and concrete echoing every which way
and people sleeping in doorways and
avocado pits sprouting in windows
of an immigrant soup shop where you sip
their signature drink a mint lemonade
before seeing your second shrink
of the afternoon a born-again
surrealist spilling dreamy poems
of abstruse association not unlike
his practice of teasing the dreams
out of his clients the better
for them to direct
unlike notes floating nowhere
directed by no one so taste
the icy greenness of your drink

::

Now let us be French for a few hours,
lounging before the day's downwinding dinner
with another brew to cool the wild soul fires that drive
you to stop at Walgreen's for backup instruments
in case you run out of ink.

There is comfort in timelessness,
sipping customers at cocktail hour in any era,
the alcohol content eternal as the echoes of Echo Park
not far from the Hollywood Freeway which leads anywhere
when headlights and taillights are not stacked on screens
like electric snakes in darkest Los Angeles.

Your fries are less than French,
your kisses not even that—you are down
to the last dish, last meal before they throw the switch,
and are trying to taste, to savor whatever's left.

::

The ale is too hoppy for a dropout of this vintage,
his tolerance lopsided because of compromised imbalances
in his melancholy index, which weighs depressively
on his joie de vivre. Time alone weighs a ton
when waiting is all there is and all you can do
is drink to stay in the mood for doom. Ha ha,
even the snaky music leaking from the speakers
is a gift.

::

The ducks have it made and don't even know it, swimming in the fountain in the park across Sunset from the Beverly Hills Hotel, traffic humming past, me and another nothing-doer on benches in the warm shade of a 75-degree day due for a high in the 80s on the brink of winter, a couple of nannies with kids and nothing else of note except the trees most of whose names beyond the palms and magnolias I don't know, so can I be said to have seen them once I've got up and gone? The drone of motors is constant, as is the pointless drive to hold some moment, however mundane, in time. What drove me to this, what's in it for me, what's left to say about anything? It's all been said and done as far back as Ecclesiastes and what good did it do him or the long-gone Greeks who cut through everything with the grief and wit of their insight.

::

A pile of rocks in the empty office park
is the only place for an old man to sit
feeling the gentle 90-degree breeze
and admiring the small trees
punctuating the parking lots
and appreciating the desert
quiet of the holiday
where he is the only one
present to hear the distant hum
of the 101 under the silent wisps
of cirrus streaking the faint
blue sky scored here and there
by jet trails, no circling hawks
to speak of, nor cougars skulking
unseen through what's left
of the brush at midday
in the suburbs where
families gather to thank
the natives for handing over
their land. Hollywood
cowboys and Indians
no longer lope over these wastes
as in my childhood when
I was the first person.

::

This town brings out my incoherence—
too much to process too fast, mixed media
messaging nonstop, messing with one's message
center, which is jammed so you can't tell
who calls and your whole house of cards
falls apart and you can't unscramble
your eggs in one skillet and you are licked.

::

Living years of one's life in six lanes of backed-up traffic
in the course of routine travels across the megalopolis
which continues to metastasize
is wrong—and so the renegade escapes again
having run out of primal friends to lunch with
and reconstruct what is lost.
The road is long but it ends in lasagna
and Sam Cooke piped in from the afterlife.

November 20–24, 2017

Last Call

Who is that cat
on the far wall
sipping a drink
served "up," from a
glass on a slim stem
with celery green, lime
green liquid, slightly
icy on a spring night,
or nearly, the stream
of storms easing a
little toward mid-
March with land-
slides in its wake,
and sunken roads
indefinitely closed,
trees crashing through
roofs, blackouts,
rivers rising and
spilling into living
rooms leaving a film
of slime, of black
mold, and now a
warming trend with
people filling the
streets, eating in
loud rooms, sipping
drinks at bars after
the kitchens close
because it is too soon
to go home alone
after the movie,

seen solo, at the
senior discount, a
perk of endurance,
as are the few
words left when
night slopes into
closing notebooks
and the last drop
of consolation is
downed.

Meeting Your Shrink for a Drink

Meeting your shrink for a drink,
what could go wrong? Are your dreams leaving you
in need of an explanation for your erection?
It is only a sign that you are still alive
in the morning of one more day of no relief
for what you thought you needed,
a sensitive interpreter of your subterranean hungers
for what or whoever is unrevealed at dawn, the face
of her you miss most, unexpectedly exposed
across a counter, a bar or cash register
behind which eyes and a shy smile brightly shine
for a few seconds, serendipitous, a flash
of refreshed pleasures remembered
even if never again made flesh, embodied
in the one always missing, always missed.
Your shrink could illuminate this over cocktails
if she would only return your calls, but she too
is suffering, her losses as grievous as yours
and she can't confess, must possess her bereaved
self as you do yours, a strange privilege
shared only with your most intimate interlocutor.

Inscribed on a Marble Slab

The marble slab of this bar
is not engraved with my name
and dates, so I must be alive
and tasting this savory risotto
with calamari and the Chianti
to finish it off after a Grey Goose
gimlet, very dry, in Half Moon Bay
following a Czech string quartet
in San Francisco, Dvorak
alive again via violins
and a cello grounding
the heartbeat of high spirits.
I can't take down what comes
to me fast enough, it slips past
before I can get a grip and am left
holding what I couldn't catch.
The words are as worthless
as they ever were, even inscribed
on white stone, unable to hold
anything more than a hollow
echo of what they swear
they knew, or witnessed once.

"Mouthfeel"

The wine poets have blown it
with a word to describe how wine feels
in the mouth, pitifully pedestrian
after the fruits and rocks, the smokes and grasses
of their vocabularies, they need to invent
a more accurate account of the oral
surrender of the gums—even gums
is a dumb word—to the red caress
of liquid kisses inside the place
desire cultivates in the taste
of love's hunger. For that, no lame word
will make the grade, the noun
needs to be savory sweet and
spicy at the same time, sensuous
and sensual as skin
oiled by a smooth hand on a summer day,
as hot soup on a winter night,
as buttery adjectives slathering the body.
Bésame mucho, sings the crooner,
and in her sultry tone the texture
of longing flows, a come-on
to indulge, to sip and swallow it all
knowing agony will follow
gratification, mouths feel
so much more as the sip lingers.
Can this be named?

Polite Society Poem

The poets of polite society
read their neatly wrapped epiphanies
the way my mother would like
nonthreatening and comprehensible
with helpful introductions
            whose little jokes
put the audience at ease
in the wine cellar
sipping comfortably among the stacked barrels
empathy assured with goodwill
of nice guys in soft sweaters
            and suave scarves
tucked into necks of dress shirts
whose top buttons are undone
            casually elegant
with the smooth formality of sommeliers
                        and I sip too
incredulous in my own attendance
            blue beret at a beat angle
aromatic of an old coffeehouse
                        or dive bar reeking of cigarettes
            and drunk hecklers
knocked back by tough truths
whose only solace is their ruthless music
no gentle nature to reassure
no homilies
            but the pastors
shepherds of the pastoral
and the well behaved
guide their admirers with gentility
toward the table where a pretty girl

in a little black dress with spaghetti straps
        on this cold night
sells their books with abandon

New Music

Arrived early,
orchestra tuning in deep cacophony,
audience filing in finding their seats,
ushers handing out programs, reporters pulling out notebooks
to record what is unreportable
                    but portable,
you can carry a tune in your pocket with enough practice,
echoing and reflecting on what you hear and see,
a Botticelli in the front row,
          her long rippling red locks a giveaway,
and the sounds of bows stroking long strings as the cellists
find their keys,
          the official photographer, himself a celebrity,
angling in for the best shot,
old friends schmoozing in the wide aisles,
the rows far enough apart to allow illusions
of elbow room while we are cheek to cheek
and ear to ear in lines of folding seats,
          except for mine, nobody to my right, a row of one's own
in which to listen and write, all night if so inspired,
"no recording of any kind allowed" but I am nothing
if not outside the law politely defying
official guidelines and ground rules
          while the music speaks for itself and is taken down
by a scribe incredulous at early rumblings of drums
less eloquent than the thunder they're trying to emulate,
then the clouds
          break for a bit of birdsong and a breeze
smelling of blood, hunters stalking dangerous
endangered species that might turn at any time
and devour them,

that's how fast the tables
can turn and the diner is suddenly dinner
wondering how he was consumed by what he was pursuing,
it was a sting all along,
the conductor's baton and the bows and drumsticks
conspiring to attack, to tickle, to provoke ironic rhythms
as infectious as they are fatal in the end.

Then the Steinway is rolled out and opened up,
microphone angled into its maw by a stagehand,
concertmaster fingering one note for orchestral orientation,
musicians lining up their tones for the composer,
the pianist and the Romanian maestro set to rip up
the virtuoso concerto
with aplomb, a young man's first blast at a big band masterpiece,
or maybe just a flying chance, a nice try, close but no laurels
to smoke backstage afterward, and nothing to tap the ashes in
or get stoned on,
a long series of sighs
and wild bangs on the black-and-whites,
it's all in his head, or was, and the writer has forced it
into the array of instruments and made them sound like his mind,
and it goes on like that, tracking his thoughts
and impressions, self-abstracted expressions
made concrete by execution,
and the sounds are killing me,
slamming and stabbing and pounding
my desire for pleasure to a pulp
with cosmic dissonance
to scramble whatever eggs I had left after all those frittati,
those tortillas, those omelets with too much of everything,

including drippings of the kitchen sink
          where the buckets aren't big enough
to catch it nor can ink begin to imitate its influence.

What I meant to say is what can't be said
except maybe in what I swear was Esperanto
          this morning on the car radio,
little traffic on Mission Street so early
and newspapers awaiting me at Safeway,
more information than I can use and it's only Saturday,
tomorrow is when it will weigh a ton and I'll have to tote it home
in a black bag like a dead body,
                    all the suffering in the world
spelled out in print and in pictures that blister credibility,
but you turn the page and there's a jewelry ad,
or a picture of a watch where time has stopped
as long as you're looking,
          but it's more than you can afford,
like the cost of this concerto with all its bells and whistles
way over your budget but you can't afford to get over it either,
                    it is all over you
          until it's all over.

Game Seven

Ballplayers with beards
and shaggy pageboys
wearing body armor
swing for the big money
in Game 7 above
the bar at the end
of the long season as
I nurse a pale ale because I need
something to take the edge off
Armageddon, all the time
in the world twisting
into a tightening
spiral sucked
into a drain
mirroring the moon
whose blues are inconsolable,
you can see her tears
swirling toward the same
black hole I'm staring into
for the same reasons,
in search of a sign, some way
to explain our errors
and why everything was
lost in the last inning.

PROFILES IN BEAUTY

Paisley Yours

These patterns
swirl in curves
over my slim shape
as if to accentuate
nature herself,
composed,
cool as a dill
pickle in a
refugee's
refrigerator,
my gaze
rhyming with yours
because that's
how eyes are,
finding
focus, zeroing
in on their own
reflection,
and I am
reflecting
on how our
glances met
that time
on the
street, or
meet now in
no man's land,
some magazine page
or postal
interlude
where the nudes

aren't worth a glance
but this veiled
and swathed and
shrink-wrapped dance
is worth dwelling on
or in
because we are
nowhere else
but here, lost
in the wild nuances
of style and
solitude, both of us
lonesome and a little
hungry when there is so
little
left to nibble on,
no little nipples
to taste so delicately
they become those sensitive
buttons of bliss
under your tongue,
and my wide belt
undone
reveals a bellybutton
deep enough
to drink from,
so please do sip
from my reservoir,
darling, I know
how thirsty you are
and how long
you have crawled
to find this

oasis, this
island of sanity
amid the
encroaching
madnesses, which is
why we must make
the most and best
of this lovely
moment when we are
one, found, bound
by what holds us
just long enough
to keep us
from the depths of
desperation,
waiting for the
simmering
enrichment of what
will fill our bowls
in the brief
eternity
of our last meal,
so be real, aware
of all this while
it lasts because
it won't last
long
and we must savor
every savory second
before the clock
runs out and time
swirls counter
clockwise down

the whole of
nothing that is
oblivion, our
destiny
which makes
everything so
much sweeter
than it would
be otherwise,
don't you
think?

Drinking from Your Empty Glass

The glass you left in the sink
looked clean enough to drink from

so I poured some water into it
and sipped from its curved lip

this late afternoon in April
as if kissing you sweetly though

you'd gone and I was alone
where just a few hours earlier

your touch had stirred my tears
held by a life of contained

aching for such a gift
which your absence opens

now in the rim of this glass
I taste your mouth

Old Photos

What do these images mean?
What do they prove?
That youth can be caught in a click
and held as evidence of our tragic
delinquency to abandon that flash
of imagined happiness, actually mixed
with so much misery we couldn't
take it anymore and took so long
to lose each other and the beauty
we were forever?
No more answerable now
than they ever were, such questions
to vex the sages suffering their own
tragedies and disasters, that's why
they disappeared into the mountains
or into their senior housing
with views through histories
unrecoverable even with total
recall, every kiss a missing
key to a garden gate
too late to open again.
Instead they shuffle
through shoeboxes wondering
at how lovely imagination makes
the agonies of such passions,
such attachments so rich
the long decades alone
can't sever them
and only the museums can show
what strange sense they made
in these shadowy rectangles.

Eurydice's Return

The ringer for Eurydice I saw across the room
up close doesn't resemble her at all.
She was a wishful figment of my thinking,
tricked for the countless time since the last time
she was lost to me forever. Even Catullus
couldn't recall her at the open mic
in the Eternal Return Café after hours,
the drunks oddly literate, they seem to know
the lyrics by heart, even the busgirls
reciting their translations from the Arabic
as they clear the tables. Such strange nights
in the netherworld, or wherever this is,
an all-night oasis for the possessed.

Luck Roulette

The urge is unstoppable,
but then you have to sift through what is produced—
or take it all as one work for better or worse.
Beautiful books in boxes stacked in the dark in a Westside warehouse.
The work goes nowhere, but must find some way.
Looking for words for a way out of the maze.
Waste of time with nothing better to do.
What is a poem and why does it matter.
(Matter-of-fact question with no hook.)
Julio, Luis, Georgie, Hank, Abe Cahan—
odd wallmates in my minimalist exhibition
stuck with Scotch tape so as to leave no trace.
Greg the invisible man and Wanda the woman they tried to erase
held in fixed shadows on the other wall,
hanging spirits, hovering presences, imperfect exemplars.
Good company on a grayish strange weather day,
escapist in the quietest way. It seemed to mean more
yet also less before, you couldn't be sure,
you were in the middle before your time,
you didn't know how deeply advanced, and so
you doubted your destiny even while surrendering to it.
The great love was anomalous, luck of gambled and lost
fortune betting on news, or an excuse to pose as a newsman
so you might meet. Luck so hard to believe even this much later.
Lingering aura of luck. Delicious licks of luck.
Long nights of sweet luck. Mornings of luxurious luck.
Afternoon interludes of naked luck.
Wicked, angelic, demonic, celestial luck.
Ruinous, catastrophic, devastating luck.
A golden treasury of slippery quicksilver luck.

Belaureled luck anointed with olive oil in Mediterranean sun.
You were one lucky son of a gun.
It must have been your turn, fortunate one.

No Gloves on Door Handles

I want your fingerprints
on everything you touch
so the detectives will know you've been here
even after I'm gone
as if the photographs were not enough
to prove your presence at the scene
of so many crimes of unpremeditated
trespass
boundaries breached
and privacies violated
as if your most intimate murmurs
endearments and cries had been overheard
and now examined by the investigators
to reconstruct what happened
as I have been trying to recreate
those moments to discover
how it might have turned out otherwise
and why your disappearance
remains unsolved
your gloves unfound
the feel of your long fingers
always on my back
unreachable

"Excetera"

It used to drive me crazy when you said that,
one of your many intellectual quirks,
like feminist theory, Franco-academic postmodernism,
whatever—our sex was good, and that's what mattered,
the way we fit in bed, our kisses rhyming
with the rhythms of our hips, a tender
curving sweetness smoothing the rough edges
of the everyday. After the terror of that terrible
September, we took each other for an antidote
to despair and lasted a whole year,
reading and eating in restaurants and making love
and talking and writing, the pleasures of poets.
You asked me once what part of your body
I liked best, and I caressed the curved bottom
of your back, the hollow behind your knee,
your beautiful long hands, so skilled in sewing
and stroking, inspiring my desire
to please you, but it couldn't last,
we would've killed each other,
et cetera.

Ignoramorous

The older I get
the more I miss what I don't know
and never bothered to learn

the Romans with their zingy epigrams
taken in small doses
and only in translation

the Greeks whose marbles
are not lost even though
vandalized by time

the Chinese by their streams
drinking wine with friends
lazily composing poems

but even Sundays stream past
faster than newspapers
and who has the music

to catch anything in its course
much less everything
for the record

I couldn't study hard enough
was too busy doing nothing
to notice what was going on

I thought I could read in her face
everything
that would teach us everything

and who'd've thought that
after all the ignorance
I know now

The Girl on the Swing

The girl on the swing
is tall and slim and
looks like all the girls
you ever loved
in a funhouse
mirror kind of way, her
grace as she moves
motionless in the
photo
with her hair flying
and fashion flaring
in her pants
reminds you
of everything
you ever admired
in such limbs,
not hers but
those other girls
who were yours
for a few hours
some summery
afternoon
in a room breezy
and shady with
tree light
flickering
and maybe a few birds
doo-wopping outside,
you were just lying
there
admiring her

fine lines and sexy
intelligence,
the way she laughed
in the right places
and outwitted you
with repartee
just when you thought
you were smart,
but no, she was
all over you in no time,
in a kind of eternity
there on that
platform
where you
also slept,
she was taking
you for a ride
you won't
forget
and making you
hers in a way
you never could
make her yours, and she
still swings through
your Sunday so much
like the one
you almost remember
and you are almost
there.

Beautiful Bird

You look like a beautiful bird
crossed with a Botticelli, your wiggly red hair

almost fictional in its flaming provocation,
untouchable but fetching nevertheless,

something like a memory in the mists of lost
desserts, unjust in their delicious

juxtaposition to present impossible
pleasures with sleeping beauties

whose nightmares paralyze
gratification, and so the sole trustee

is reduced to admiring every
truth he knows cannot be trusted

outside the law
of eternal return, past lives

recycling themselves with nothing
to prove but persistence

of what was never personal in the first place
beyond its intimacy.

Blackberry Pie Sonnet

Who left these sweet seeds in my teeth,
stuck so I taste them as if eternally,
like the songs caught on tape so long ago
they sprout much later and bear fruit in your smile,
elusive and fetching at the same time.
These long warm evenings just before summer
when your arms shine with long creamy light
sing melismatic romance in long whispers,
like what I'd say if I could cajole you
into coming close enough to hear.
But listen to this: a stylus scratching an old record
to bring out a thorny sound that sticks around
and leaves these lovely stains
on your sensitive fingers as you read.

Profiles in Beauty

That lovely face seen from the side
staring stupidly into her little screen
is not so appealing
and it's fitting you should see it that way
a century removed with only your eyes
and ears to witness what you don't get
after all the lost years
lucky to be found even once
now it's all here for the first time
even if out of sight
the floods of those faces
those embracing gazes
you gave yourself over to
in blind obedience and adoration
all presence and no future
for a few hours days decades
you wouldn't trade if you could retrieve them
because it would turn out the same
ages cities nations apart
mountains deserts oceans between
ink obscuring everything
because the only thing that held
what was escaping
was what could not be photographed
couldn't be recorded
only transcribed
one line at a time
like the outline of an unforgettable face
seen from an oblique
intimate angle

Long Twilight

For now, the skylight
illuminates, and I
will write until the
sky darkens and the
light on the page
fades in the falling
shadows of a May
night as the pianist
plays what songs
remain, which they
do because they are
made to outlast
the skilled hands
driving the instrument,
all those notes lost
even as they re-
sound in the mind
and stay there as if
echoing always like
some face seen up
close in dim light
once and remembered
like the embrace
sustained by adoration
and gratitude, by
devastation and the
loss of everything
but that, the sweet
melody triggering
what is missed,
bésame mucho, so

many kisses they
combine to taste
eloquent in one
mouth watering
with fruit music,
that which drips
more delicious with
each bite, its sweet-
ness slightly acidic,
which only accents
its bitter intimacy,
what nobody learned
in sex ed because it
was crossed too darkly
with heartache, with
infinite grief and
what if, what might
have been if only
time hadn't intervened
and life taken those
turns that led to such
long solitudes and
opportunities to wonder
what you might have
done to understand and
respond in real time,
changing the way
things went in that
flash of happiness
under the sign of the
Snake, which appears
only when planets
align above lives

lucky to be in one
place at a time
exactly right, some
city, let's say, where
serendipity struck
and took them both
so far from what
they thought, they
never found their
way to figure it
out, could not find
their way back and
found themselves
estranged from
their own souls,
they were so confused
by what had moved
them together that
way before breaking
them apart and
scattering them like
perfectly played notes
in some distant night
where one long stroke
or twist of blue light
as it cools revives
what never was lost
after all because
there it is in a
long twilight with
traces of Spain, dashes
of easy summers, mists
of skin whose sweat

smelled sweet enough
to lick and laughter
ensued under a spell
of magnolia shade
and citrus glow, a
squeezing and savoring
of every sip as the
sun slowly rolled
into the ocean and a
hint of night made
itself felt in the
musician's fingers
and in the stars
unfolding their
sneaky myths and
legendary tales that
never end, never
exactly resolve but
go on and on
again and again

Today

As the WALK sign blinks
counting down the seconds
she is running toward me
across Front Street
her small braless breasts
bouncing beneath her light sweater
lightly happily youthfully alive
my eyes can't help looking
she's coming right at me
and right past that close
little nipples subtly sculpted
in motion as she runs in a hurry
into and through my remembering
leaving a blur and a sweet glow

Sure Thing

Sure thing,
you're welcome,
happy to do it.

That's what I said
to the nubile beauty,
slim and blonde

in silver tights and yellow
tank top, with wiry arms
and a warm tan

trying to pick up
a free easy chair
from the sidewalk

across from the park
by Holy Cross Church
I stopped to help

while walking home
from downtown,
the two of us together

lifting it easily
into the back
of her SUV.

She was grateful
and she thanked me
as I walked away.

Being With

They're designed to arouse desire,
their bodies are meant to make you want
to mate, no wonder you can't help
noticing, as subtly as possible,
and cultivating an intense tenderness
because you can't touch such skin
anymore, nor kiss with a sensitive tongue
another tongue like hers again
ever, so all you can do is thank Pan
you can remember that much sweet
luck in your life, and can imagine
her in these others, and be with them
some afternoon like this with a light
breeze, lying together in the remembering mind.

Brainy Girls

I am in love with all the brainy girls
their sexy thinking seduces me every time
their talk about everything is so intelligent
their letters are full of touching revelations
even their emails are intimate
and back in the days of face-to-face conversation
before the age of the prophylactic mask
to see their lips as they spoke
so crisply and smartly
and to catch a dazzling glimpse of their eyes' brightness
was to feel a tender bondage
laced with a sweet pain of longing
to be one with each of them
and polyamorous with all
this plural intimacy is not promiscuous
but a deeply selective
adoration and gratitude
for shared understanding
the brainy girls are the women I grew up to love
at impossible distances
and closenesses

LITTLE SYMPHONIES

The Perfect Poem

The perfect poem is where you want to live
lingering in each line as you read
through to the end and then read again
gaining more of its music and its meaning
in circular motions that move through you
leaving a little residue to reside
somewhere inside where it remains
by heart where you have it when you need it
but you can't live there it lives in you
as long as you retain those lines
moving in circles in your mind in time
spheres of influence where you find rhymes
arriving in rhythm as the world turns
as if it were a place where you could live

What Is Expressed

What is expressed
is not oneself
not anyone's and yet
something is revealed
laid bare
that is inescapable
unmistakable
traces of what you are
or were in the few hours
it seemed you needed
to set down what
you didn't know
it would be a way
to hold the uncontainable
in space that would fit
someplace
some page where hardly
anyone would find some
trace of earned ignorance
and that unknown
didn't hurt as much as
you were told
it was more like a joke
you didn't get
and that's how
you learned
to laugh at what
you missed

Radio Madness

My voices echo yours,
we hear them in the dark
whispering sweet everythings all at the same times
in eternal turnings that recur in cycles
and remind us our minds are together again
even after flying different ways
to discover the same truths
now broadcast to anyone who is listening.
We stop to hear the roses unfolding,
slowly exploding to share their rare scents,
blushing like the face of her we are flirting with
for the first time—
we've just met and are suddenly intimate
in the rush of recognition, a gift
we don't even know who to thank for.
These rare nights when waves range through skies
to arrive subtly inside our privacies and touch us
are what we live for now,
bereft of so much we've lost.
Listen and know
how alone we are, bound
by unspeakable understandings.
We've been there and we savor what we've learned,
not for the pain but what came later,
our unwritten worlds made one
in spoken words. This is how
we touch and are comforted.

Is This Necessary?

Maybe not but you never know.
Something wants to be said
despite whatever evidence against,
whatever audience does not exist,
whatever interlocutor is missing.
Could I call at this hour anyway
even if I had her number
inked on my arm
and one of those devices to stream the lines
I would say if I knew how
in a soft tone no one could mistake
for pathos? I would go on at length
in search of a dénouement, which is French
for unraveling, falling apart, coming undone
as coming does. You want to murmur whispering
intimacies to bring her into your rite
of understanding when so much confounds,
befuddles, fails to make sense or make anything
you can stabilize or erase even with a touch,
a kiss.
It seemed, once, that could be done
and was a kind of redemption
but it didn't work out however many years
of bondage you endured
and now you are escaped
and lost in a landscape of your own making.
Such are the circles
the dizzy design, the wounded
stagger through on fire,
the ones with nothing else to do
find solace in.

Nude Self-portrait in Barbershop Mirrors

There's nothing here to hide behind.
Whatever you could make up would be true.
Fact-check your disbelief at the door
to the funhouse where the ride
will drive you into the dark
with no way out but deeper into the dark
of mirrors testing the limits
of reflection. You are exposed
coming and going, and the man whose blade
is at your throat is you, easily opening a vein
while at the same turn of the skilled wrist
styling your vanity to reveal only
what you want to see—
but anyone can see through that
at a glance, so transparent
are your evasions and diversions, your
pretexts and pretenses,
even your parts of speech stamped
with your indelible brand.
You were sold on something that wasn't there,
a self you could claim, the selfsame
self of the controlled spill
you believe may relieve
the pressure behind your floodgates
before the whole landscape of your illusions
is utterly subsumed with what you can't contain.
It's you, your naked truth, your self-
inflicted portrait, your beautiful
wound.

Little Symphonies

Somebody pushing a cart
or rolling a suitcase up High Street
on a Tuesday night at 10:45, no sirens
faint car hum on Highway 1
fine ringing in old ears
tinnitus
too much rock and roll in stoned youth
string quartets my preference now
or silence passing for music
filled with Cagelike sounds
rustle of *New York Times* stuffed into recycling
my little symphonies
philharmonic listenings to nothing
scratch of Uni-ball Signo gel grip
on notebook pages scored at a discount
in last days of Logos, closing
loss of an irreplaceable
bookstore sanctuary
soon to be a brewery run by a church, no joke
downtown now
the houseless bed down in doorways
sidewalks hosed off in the morning
stores of stylish clothes,
outdoor cafés,
customers on computers,
mesmerizing devices,
my daily rounds, my nightly
exercise
trying to find the sounds

that say what is
          unknown
lone voice in the street, late

Museum

Now that these walls are well-hung with the evidence
it is almost a relief to be imprisoned
in the museum displaying the mementos
of your memory, it is memorable
and memorial in the extreme to muse on
these unique or all but unique
artifacts, which oddly contain the fictions
of your existence.
But you're still alive,
or were last time you looked,
but maybe when you woke late
this morning from a lost dream
it was into another life
and you are gone
into these rooms where everywhere you turn
a face breaks your heart with its beauty
or a work of art reminds you of its maker.
Even the sirens outside don't pull you
past the windows because the light
falls just so on everything inside
and at this time of day it glows
because it's getting dark and this is the last chance
to reflect that light before it goes,
and the curves of the bowls
and the lines in the black-and-white photos
remind you of those immortal forms
you tried to save
and so you curated this collection
in search of something less ephemeral.

::

To live in beauty,
Bonnie Margolis told me,
is the best you can do when love
has broken you. We were looking out
from her funky trailer at the view
of the coast above Anchor Bay
where I had just arrived
to recover from my devastation,
and my eyes tried to drink in
those green slopes down to the ocean a mile away
and the whitecaps farther out in the bluescape
thrashed by wind
and clouds pinkening on the horizon beyond
because to think of what I'd lost
was too much to take
or take in
faced with the emptiness ahead
in bed where she should have been.
Even now, so many dramas downstream,
I can't quite believe we've moved on
and so must settle for this, this view
of a body of water
instead of hers.

::

Modigliani's nudes and stylishly dressed
austere young models relaxed in the light
of red wine brighten every room
as if they too were girlfriends
so bonded to you they stayed on
and made a seraglio of your cell,
a sensuous monastery with one monk

in residence, docent of his own
long celibacy. He remembers when
he took the vow he thought he was signing up
for something else, and now he's stuck
like a skeleton in his own closet,
he can't help himself, he is all bones
with echoes of old whispers
and moans and tastes of a quick tongue
as remnants of flesh
and even that feels good.

Pandora's Shoebox

Photographs, passports, portraits of the artist at assorted ages,
friends, loves looking ever more beautiful, lean arms locked around his neck,
draped in langorous ease over his shoulders, eyes' calm gaze graced instantly
and ever after in the click that caught them like that,
desires gratified for a while and impossible to satisfy always,
dramas of lost bliss, anger, anguish, jealousy, despair, longing, conflict,
romantic agitation faded with the fog of all those years, nights, hours
possessed by what he thought he had that was never his,
elusive flavor of a youthful mouth, lips the curved shape of yeses,
the whole mess of a long life slipped into plastic sleeves
and stashed in a bottom drawer
unpacked to decorate the last stop
where all is exhibited, exposed to the all-eroding flow
even as it is held, holding traces of where he was once
and with whom—sweet and bitter phantoms, companions, absences
whose grieving never ceases—fixed shadows, chaotic forces
loosed from a cardboard box.

Sweeping the Courtyard

Pulling a stiff push broom over the cracked concrete,
sweeping the scattered leaves of yesterday's blustery gusts,
listening to the scratchy rhythm, breathing the stray dust
unsettled by my good housekeeping, I'm starting the new year
like a young monk assigned by the master to the lowliest
enlightenment imaginable, and I like it, this unskilled task,
the subtlety of its simplicity, taking the space in sections,
dropping the debris in the plastic buckets to be dumped
in the yard-waste recycling carts, a few scraps of foil
and flakes of old white paint mixed in with the organic matter,
teaching me patience and the pleasures of imperfection,
a meditation more meaningful than sitting still
because it accomplishes what I didn't know I wanted
to do, clearing the fresh space for doing nothing.

Mourning Dove

One of our courtyard doves,
whose mate I spotted in their nest this morning
in the rain gutter under the awning,
crashed into the plate glass front door
and landed on the veranda in a bloody mess
I found on my way out to walk downtown for my newspapers.
The corpse of the bird, its shattered skull bleeding
through the eye as it lay face down on the painted concrete,
scattered feathers and bloodstains in an arm's-length radius
splattered as if by an explosion, made for a tough start
for this Fourth of July, otherwise so pleasantly quiet
with a fog-cooled breeze coming off the bay
as the sun breaks through and shines warmly on the terrace
now that I'm back with my papers puttering about,
transplanting a few succulents clipped from the front landing,
coming full circle back to the dead bird,
whose remains I spent a half hour cleaning up
and scrubbing with all-purpose cleaner and an old
t-shirt stained with come from long-ago masturbations.
Now instead of stroking my cock I spill this ink
from the tip of the Uniball as a way of relieving, releasing
my desperate love, grieving and remembering my dead dove.

Stone Face

It looks Mexican
like something from the anthropology museum
old and handcarved in hard gray-greenish jade
staring with empty eyes
pleasantly heavy in the hand
picked up for 15 bucks at the Antique Faire
the seller ignorant of its origins
its provenance an estate sale
somebody died and left it for dead
rescued by chance
and now I can't stop looking at it
marveling at its hard beauty
its flat-nosed antiquity
its ancient grief
one more stunning object
for my collection
my memorial museum
where I am the curator and the curated
of a history that won't quit
though it feels so over there's nothing left
but artifacts
almost convincing evidence
things happened
people came and went
loves   friends   family
even most of me gone
into these pictures
these lines in a book
ancient faces in stone

Columbus Day

Is the root of colonize Colón?
Or is that just history and language
rhyming? Words have a way
with themselves, they insist on saying more
or less what you ever meant,
what couldn't be said
without embarrassment, nakedness
of the dream where you are reading
your heart out to a big crowd
but you forgot to bring your book
and have to improvise but you're
speechless, like those sailors
coming ashore to a new world.
But to the natives it was old already
and what was new were the intruders
in strange clothes and everything
suddenly changed, all ways
of life began to unwind
in the ill winds, time unraveling,
accelerating like wildfire
over the dry hills and across
the tragically discovered and soon to be
consumed land. How it all happened
even the professors can't explain,
they confess it's too much
to get their heads around,
it happened so fast.

Just Another Siren Song

Should I go see the feminist strippers tonight,
Sin Sisters Burlesque, and enjoy from a great distance
the sexy jokes and sweaty skin of the entertainers,
or mix with the masses at the Greek Festival,
Sapphic cuisine and Aegean dances Homeric in their perennial
blue hues, a sea of people I don't know if I want to see or be with,
too many bodies and souls trying to have a good time
while there is time. My sirens have strapped me
lest I be made a sap of by their succulence,
their irresistible sweet and smoky nothings
whispered across choppy waters while I writhe
in ecstatic disbelief, so delicious is their unreachable sound.
Or more intimate yet should I stay here and see how deep
my unspeakable desires can be indulged without witnesses
or deprived once more of their darkest need.

Balcony Poem

The corrugated roof of the garage across the way
	adjacent to the carport with solar panels
is a dried-blood rusty red under a haze-blue sky
	beneath shadowy eucalypts on the hill behind
and the sounds of Saturday spring evening
	traffic ripped intermittently by motorcycles
and delicately threaded with birdsong
	and mountains in the distance topped by radio towers
whose red lights will begin blinking as night falls,
	a strange landscape rippling with contradictions, torn
that way and this by crosscurrents of pleasure
	and melancholy, subtle sad smile of the bookstore clerk
across the counter on a sunny morning
	when she'd rather be in bed with her boyfriend,
succulents are my witness
	swollen with April rain under the red tiles
that rhyme with the rust in front and frame the view,
	the lone dove's cool calls atop the power pole,
noises of cars on the business route,
	musings in shades of blue.

View

The view eludes me,
morning sun so blind
I can't even raise
the shade, and once
it's risen above the
roof the sky is so
unstable as to be
indescribable, its
floating shapes of
various whites and
grays refusing to
stay still, submit
to being fixed,
no slipping twice
in the same wakes
of birds rowing by
or riding the breeze
as if designed to
sail lightly and
leave their admirers
speechless, unable
even to trace a
sketch of their
effortless trajectory—
that's why I write.

Lost Highway Poem

How easily along the
highway the poem
flows with no radio
to crowd out sound
so you can hear the
language in your
head that rhymes
with the landscape
and you let it go

Still Life with Newspapers and Calendulas

The stack of unread news on the tile table
grows higher and deeper, its aging ink
heavier as the days fade and darkness climbs
into the tired brains exhausted by nightmares,
gangsters in the saddle galloping
toward cliffs of no return,
no good guys to bring them down,
to drag them back from the brink—
yet those yellow and orange flowers
in the blue-rimmed Mexican glass
on the Spanish tiles
please the eye even in this half-light
when the Saturday night sirens
are silent for now
and only the rumbling motors on Highway 1
can be heard above the moans
of missing loves. Listening to those
intimate rhythms in the remote closeness
pumps brightness into the calendulas
and into the photographs
of lost faces, so many stories
asleep in the pile of pages,
days old, new night no match
for the enduring absences.

A Murder of Crows on Christmas Day

A black and squawky Christmas to you, too, birds,
        flapping past making a racket and hanging briefly in the trees
on High Street just off Highway 1 lined by a row of eucalypts,
        waves of talkative corvids of various sizes
and ages and pecking and yakking orders,
        hundreds, thousands headed toward the coast,
maybe over Escalona where Daniela dwells,
        or over Western Drive and Nicole's house,
both of whom broke my heart thirty years apart,
        leaving me to stare out at the sky from my airy terrace
and wonder what conversations are in those wires
        paused on by the crows tapping into them with their feet
and taking away a little electricity
        to power their garrulous voices as they sweep west.
I meant to make lunch but I was torn outdoors
        to get a load of this raucous spectacle
under a light gray sky
        with mountains outlined across the bay
and traffic taking a sabbatical
        to better allow to be heard the murder of crows.

Jalapeño Poem

The jalapeño is a dependable pepper.
You can have your serranos, your
hot-as-hell habaneros, your cherry bombs,
your padróns, your poblanos, your shishitos,
your Anaheims and Fresnos, your red and yellow bells,
but I'll take the humble jalapeño
for its taste, its kick, its versatility
pickled in escabeche or chopped fresh
for an omelet or a stir-fry
with rice or whatever else,
not even necessarily Mexican.
Just this afternoon I simmered
an inch of chopped jalapeño
with onion crescents, a garlic tooth
and half a dozen leaves of rainbow chard
until they were ready in the cast-iron skillet
sizzling with bacon fat and olive oil
for the farmers market eggs
scrambled with a fork and poured into the pan
for a Mediterranean lunch
at a Mediterranean hour
on a Mediterranean day
above the bay across which
I can see Monterey,
a cool recumbent profile purpling the horizon.
Such moments, spiked with the seeds and
crunchy flesh I can still taste
an hour later, still savor
like a kiss on the remembering tongue,
are a balm for the blues in bad times.

Shine on, Harvest Moon

Lotta people sleeping on the sidewalk tonight,
tents pitched and piles of stuff spread out alongside the post office
just at dusk, big moon coming up over the mountains
and first fall chill calling for a scarf.

Lots of other folks are out for a good time,
running into friends at concerts, ordering drinks,
spending good money in restaurants because good times
are running out, weather has gone rogue and dark rockets
are hovering just over the lost horizon.

How sweet to taste this kiss then
knowing it may be the last one, it feels like it lasts longer than ever
like the cadenza at the end of a song that brings you to tears,
grieving and grateful for what it dredges up,
all that sunken love deep-sixed long since
that suddenly staggers you with its tragedy

though you know it is only the species'
need to reproduce that seduced you,
proving you're an animal above all
no matter your aspirations.

How you got even this far is inexplicable,
like each of these others' path to the unforeseen.

Overnight Letter

You are too good
for your own good,
giving everything so many times over
you have lost count
of the lives saved by your kindnesses,
those listenings and the light words
spoken rightly.
And still you study
the books of those who know
so much less they have to write it down
while you remain ignorant
of your wisdom and say it anyway
for no reason. These ironies
turn us inside out with their reversals
of impossible understanding,
no way out of both/and
everywhere, and escapist art
leading only deeper
into the bottomless
unknown
where we swim and drink
its endless gifts, refreshed.
My vigilance after midnight
writes in your sleep
that you may dream in streams of unconsciousness,
pure being, pure nothing
one and the same.
What you knew all along.

What never explained itself.
What leads you on
neverendingly.

—for L.

Discourse on Distraction

Distraction is inspiration,
the incidental a symptom of destiny
when synchronism and coincidence coincide
and surprising parallels and intertwinings
combine to create abstract-appearing patterns
that are in fact figurative, depicting the shapes of faces
if you listen closely between the lines, life drawings
of nudes you knew when first you were a student
of these elusive arts, the subtle glance,
the warm gleam in the quietly smiling lips,
the melody of the almost familiar song.
What you heard on the street is true,
those blues the busker was crooning
and the sweet greeting of that girl
you didn't recognize but who knew you and remembered,
the bearded disheveled one yelling his objection
to your gait as you stride by—
there is no escaping the script you write with every step,
the strange rhymes ringing amid the dissonance,
the gifts, the great griefs,
the peripheral visions.

Dyspossessions

I gave the pictures away,
had no more space to fit them in my albums,
and gave away the discs with the engraved music,
I had nothing to play them on,
then went the scraps on which had been scribbled
notes so gnomic no one could understand
followed by the clothes stolen from my wife's closet
in case I ever transcended sex
but I never did so I gave them away

and that was just the beginning, I was just getting started
stripping away what I thought
at one time worth saving
but it proved illusory, I was whistling through my beret
walking past the pyres on which my old loves lay smoking,
my sweetest memories taken for what they weren't
by the tone-deaf and by those with agendas
who took my tender gratitude
for bragging, but I kept on

disposing of my possessions, I had to lose
whatever I had in order to find
what I needed, it was contradictory
and more perverse than paradoxical
but increasingly pointless,
what I was getting at or trying to get
beyond was beyond me, no matter
what I shed it was out of reach,
I couldn't figure out what it was

and I was disappearing, fading in every mirror,
slipping out of the picture until my signature
I'd carved in the floor with a penknife
purchased for that purpose
was all that remained, which no one could read
anymore, so possessed by their stuff
in which they could scarcely see
even themselves, let alone
what was left of me.

IRENE BABLÉ MARRUFFI

CONFINAMIENTO :: LOCKDOWN

Though fear will always have more arguments, choose hope.

SENECA

Miedo

No tengo miedo a enfermar. Tal vez,
quisiera haber enfermado ya y poderlo contar,
bailar bajo el paraguas de anticuerpos deseados.
Mientras, por los cristales de mi ventana
observo la lluvia de días sin salida,
horas difuminadas en un tiempo desterrado.

Tengo miedo a lo que puede cambiar
sin mi consentimiento, estando sin estar.
Observo mi construcción de la vida
frágil como un castillo de naipes,
etérea como este viento que revuela
el horizonte descarado e inconsciente.

Aún siento más miedo por la inutilidad
de tantas muertes sin consuelo,
por el agotador ritmo de los respiradores
en gargantas ahogadas por la enfermedad.
Que todo el esfuerzo habrá sido en vano
y el horror sea nuestro tesoro silencioso.

Fear

I'm not afraid of getting sick. Maybe
I'd like to have been sick and could tell the story,
dancing under the umbrella of desired antibodies.
Meanwhile I'm watching the rain run down
the window glass these days with no way out,
blurry hours in a time of exile.

I'm afraid of what can change
without my consent, of being without being able to be.
My life looks to me
fragile as a card castle,
ethereal as this wind swirling
shameless across the oblivious horizon.

I feel even more afraid for the uselessness
of so many deaths with no consolation,
for the exhausting rhythm of the ventilators
down throats drowning in illness.
That all our strength has been in vain
and that horror will be our silent treasure.

Soledad

Dentro del vacío que la soledad dibuja
todas las certezas parecen difuminarse.
Cotidianeidad abortada por números
incesantes de labios enmudecidos.
Silencio y aislamiento se entrelazan
para relatar la incertidumbre del mañana.
La taquicardia sostiene el pecho asomado
a calles despojadas de transeúntes
y casi no puedes creer que la ficción
sea más real que la nube de tu mañana.

Solitude

Inside the void solitude sketches
every certainty looks smudged.
Ordinariness disrupted by so many
endless numbers of muted mouths.
Silence and isolation intertwine
whispering their doubts about tomorrow.
Your chest leaning out over the abandoned
street is kept alive by tachycardia
and you almost can't believe fiction
could be more real than your clouded future.

Desconfianza

La posibilidad del contagio está en los ojos de todos los encuentros.
Acurrucada en la pupila, negra y profunda la desconfianza.
Se han infectado todas las relaciones, incluso el beso de la madre.

Las fórmulas matemáticas predicen con aires de pitonisas
el día estimado de tu próximo abrazo, fugaz como la estrella
a la que pediste un deseo sin poder cobrar esa esperanza.

Se enredan las raíces que te ataban a la tierra, misteriosa
y profunda la espera de los días con ritmos nuevos,
escribiendo una partitura de silencios inesperados
sobre las rutas matutinas de las antiguas horas punta.

Ahora mides los metros de tu salvación, escéptico a las noticias
con ese falso optimismo con el que has borrado tu sonrisa.

Distrust

The chance of contagion is in the eyes of everyone you meet.
Deep black distrust curled up in the pupils.
All our relations have been infected, including the mother's kiss.

Mathematical formulas predict with the air of soothsayers
the approximate date of your next embrace, fleeting as the star
your desire wished on, powerless to harvest that hope.

The roots that bound you to the earth are tangled, deeply
mysterious the waiting through days moving to new rhythms,
writing a score of unexpected silences
over the morning routes of the fixed hours.

Now you're taking the measure of your salvation, skeptical of the news
with that false optimism you've used to erase your smile.

Epidemiología

Cuando hayamos dado una vuelta al Sol sabremos lo útil
del sacrificio compartido de tantas largas noches insomnes,
a la espera del pronóstico del parte cifrado de la enfermedad.
Dentro de mi casa se respira la libertad—sin mascarilla—
y el barrio sostiene su aliento con músicas y aplausos compartidos.
Nos reencontramos en entramados de páginas web olvidadas.
¿Acaso tenemos más tiempo? Acaso se ha desperdigado
y lo estamos recogiendo poco a poco, como las piezas de un puzle
que pensabas acabar hace años y ahora descansa en el caos
de sus fragmentos, como tus horas y los temores, sin un rumbo.
Con los proyectos desordenados por un virus
que sucumbe a las leyes matemáticas de la epidemiología:
el contagio es la infección de nuestra red de relaciones.

Epidemiology

When we've made one trip around the sun we'll understand what use
was the shared sacrifice of all the long sleepless nights,
waiting for a sign from disease's coded reaches.
Freedom can breathe in my house—without a mask—
and the neighborhood breathes with music and shared applause.
We meet in frames of forgotten web pages.
Maybe we have more time? Maybe it's scattered
and we're collecting it bit by bit, like jigsaw pieces
we thought we'd put together years ago now spread in the chaos
of the puzzle's fragments, like your hours and fears, directionless.
With plans derailed by a virus
obeying epidemiology's mathematical laws:
contagion is the infection of our network of relations.

PANDEMIC CADENZA

Ringing It In

Why am I not sleepy at midnight on New Year's Eve
when I've been sleeping so badly all these weeks
and explosions are going off downtown,
everyone out there trying to have a good time,
sounds of bombs and gunshots to celebrate
a random click of the clock, sounds of rockets
sizzling through the sky, faint voices yelling
by the Town Clock where the cops are watching
for drunks getting out of hand under the floodlights,
a desperate night as the oceans rise
and fires close in on the cities
and waves of racists and fascists mount their thrones
to rule as presidents for life while the stateless
bed down in squalid camps at the borders
waiting for doctors and lawyers who never arrive
and homeless addicts set off fireworks
because a horrible year is over
and another even worse one has begun
and I should be tired but the itching keeps me alert
and the more I scratch the more it itches
so maybe I'll stay up reading and writing all night
but probably not because I'm already tired
of the effort, the futile exercise, the stupidity
of the noises in the street and the sounds streaming
through my head and down my arm into my hand
and through the Uni-ball Signo onto this page.

1/1/2020

Dark Dahlias

Dahlias the thick dark color of cabernet
bought on impulse at the farmers market the other day

are starting to wither in the Italian pitcher
scored at a yard sale years ago in Gualala

the succulents in pots on the terrace need some attention
transplants to bigger pots, soil amendments, more room to bloom

I will go on spraying the aphids as needed
I will cook my soups and compose salads

and whip up smoothies
in these purgatorial days of existential suspense

no telling what's next in the epic serial
of one day after another dealing new twists

in the dealt hands of hopeless gamblers
playing our last chips with no lucky lady

she has struck out on her own adventure
moved by young male muses

those handsome dudes have everything
and they're giving her what she needs

not an ace up your sleeve nor switchblade in your sock
will get you out of this mess

the whole casino is a house of cards in a hurricane
your hand blown every wrong way

with horrors around every corner and no secret
annex nor righteous benefactor to protect you

and even if your private luck holds out
the world around is beyond repair

that's why these gloomy flowers will have to do
brightening the day with their wine-dark light

Everywhere You Look Is Beauty

Everywhere you look is beauty
anything you say could be cliché
          and who cares
you are free to be an idiot
          as Duncan taught
you are free to worship
the jaded lady
with fan on the bookcase
with the Bose radio
          playing a fado anthology
paintings by friends
          two out of three gone
part of the beauty
everywhere in sight
on Friday night
no sirens to speak of
          because of curfew
                    it's past 10
no one is to be found out
          and if so fined
and so we are ensconced
locked down till dawn
and where would we go anyway
          silence or music
                    it's a tough call
when screaming is what is called for
gnashing of teeth
ripping of too-tight shirts
                    torn by tattooed arms
wailing weeping
working out on machines

taking classes online
composing odes
anything to sublimate
        the sublime aching to break through
the simplicity
of deathlessness
devastating memory
        on the rampage always
smell of soup
        everywhere you breathe
                so feel it and smell
dark air out there
time running out
words not enough
        but that's all that's left after the vast
                subtraction
along with a few figures
like the jade lady
and the tin lion assemblage
and the Nicaraguan kids
snapped in passing
        on the back of a truck
on a gray day
otherwise long gone
as now will be
before you knew it was here
when we can't catch what we don't know
        nor hit what we can't see
how does baseball always
        find its way
everywhere you think
        like Fat Jack's aphorisms
You don't want to have to go begging hat in hand

All you have to sell is confidence
Roll with the punches
You gotta get your scars
            and your Cuban cigars
which killed him at 75
and he too keeps coming back
because what comes
                    is out of control
I'm coughing I need a drink
            a sip or two
of Pellegrino will do
when you have nothing to do
and you do it anyway

Sunflowers

The sunflowers look almost apologetic
for being so happily yellow in these dark nights
but the days despite the enforced isolation
are kind with their warm blue shining
streak of bay beyond the rooftops
ablaze like silver at the end of November

the afflictions are neverending
and the luck equally inexplicable
those who are spared the worst
or mated and stuck with a sweetheart
perform experiments in coexistence
or solo simply in paying attention

these black-eyed flowers in the Spanish pitcher
grown far elsewhere and flown in
give small joys
when they are bold enough to be noticed
but you must open your eyes
to meet theirs and see yourself

New Year, New Day

On the big balcony
with the big garden of succulents
            in pots on pallets
                        on bricks
and the rock garden flowing
around the birdbath
by the concrete Buddha
and the rusted horseshoe cat
                        with wire whiskers
            smiling

two scrub jays
regular visitors
alight while I'm out here
            reading *The New York Times*
one by one
they check out the birdbath
            not six feet away

I stay still
until one dips in
            happily splashing about
                        and yakking
Thanks! or *Happy New Year!*
or just *Hey this feels great!*
            hopping to the rail
                        fluffing its feathers
then back to the bath
            to splash and laugh
again and again

cool sun through high clouds
Monterey across visible through mist
hum of light traffic on Highway 1
fizzwater at hand
beautiful newspaper
overdue rain in the forecast
good leftovers in the fridge
letters on the desk
locked down alone
in domestic bliss

so far so good

1/1/2021

Who We Are

The people who hid for years during World War II
to keep from being sent to the camps,
the people who were caught and sent to the camps,
the refugees from this or that war,
this or that famine, drought, hurricane, murderous gang,
sleeping in squalid fields on the border of a country
where they're not welcome,
mentally ill people sleeping in tents under a freeway,
people imprisoned for possessing marijuana,
for political dissidence, for speaking,
poisoned for leading the opposition,
beheaded for reporting on the grievances of the beheaders,
people exiled and grieving for their lost land,
people evicted with their stuff piled on the sidewalk,
people sleeping in cars between shifts at minimum-wage jobs,
people who caught the plague in some lost century,
all the different plagues that have thinned humanity
so that people could have more sex and make more children
to ravage the planet with their advances in consumption,
people who have used up the planet
and run out of what to ruin—
we could be any of them
and are, only a little luckier
in our ergonomic easy office chairs
assembled ourselves from a video;
we could be ourselves on medication
without which our madness would be manifest
instead of contained for fear of incarceration;
we could be in mourning for the undoing
of democracy, the dismantling of institutions,
the lynchings of ancestors,

the trashing of the Capitol by hooligans
and plainclothes Nazis
and nostalgics for the lost Confederacy
dragging their flags across the marble floors
and taking selfies with the ashamed statues—
we are all of these because we are everything
we never expected to be.

The Night Before I Turn Seventy-four

I'm listening to Pablo Casals
play Bach on the Bose player
          instead of news
residues of which
the music cleanses

inside history you need to know
what's going on but don't kill yourself
          with information
it will still be there
after a break

almost my dad's age
when he died
I'm still alive
          the same as ever
                    almost
except for the plague
          and the lockdown
                    and the reactionary attack
on democracy
          and reality
by the "very special"

I miss my place of worship
          Kuumbwa Jazz
and movies at the Nickelodeon
          and happy hour at Lúpulo
gabbing with a friend
admiring the transient beauties
          over beers and tacos

ordinary pleasures

but I have more than enough
          for now
in my film noir Mediterranean aerie
          with a half-dozen masks
The New York Times
friends' books
friends' paintings
friends closer than ever
                    thanks to distance

I swear I saw
dark brown eyes
brown-skinned cheekbones
dark brown hair with chestnut highlights
above a black mask
and intelligent sentences
spoken by a mouth
I couldn't see
          and I wasn't dreaming

such mixed messages
paradoxical double binds
          old age young desires
drunk with poems and romance
blasted and blissed out
on beauty

these are the wild dark wordless thoughts
          the cello speaks

Vaccination

When I pull off the bandage it itches a little.
That's it. No blood. A barely perceptible dot
where the needle went in, which I scarcely felt.
Something was in the syringe, some thick liquid,
colorless, containing some patented potion
whose task is to outwit a spiky virus
that keeps evolving, changing, mutating
the better to evade the antibodies, but now my body
with new antibodies has a fighting chance
to intercept and neutralize the pathogen.
We'll see how immune this makes me,
see how sick I don't get when exposed,
see what happens when I kiss the one
whose touch I've missed for endless years
of not being touched except by nurses with needles
drawing my blood into small vials
to be sent to the lab to be tested for every disease,
or nurses with needles injecting my arm with vaccine
so I could be touched again, so I could hug someone
someday if I got the chance,
so I could sit unmasked
some night in a restaurant
and see the naked laughter of my companion.
Laughing, singing, speaking are high-risk behaviors,
like having sex in a bathhouse with a stranger
and in this desperate attempt at intimacy
catching your death.
But now you can breathe
outdoors, looking at the sky, its clouds' celestial shapes,
prophetic permutations of illusions

of protection, of immunity,
of a mystery future
you may live to meet.

Pandemic Cadenza

That's what you call the last notes
cascading over the last cliffs
into the abyss at the bottom
of the epidemic
Pan only knows
everything and says
nothing so we're left
counting our casualties
like statisticians
calculating bottomless losses
this is what we live for
to be devastated
with gratitude for what we had
before it vanished like all the years
even last year
with its horrors
and disasters that seem
never to end
falls streaming
precipitously
over immense rock
perpetually perennially
redundantly
because it's been said
already and there's nothing
to add but you go on
because that's all
you know how to do
like Nagg in the trashcan
or was it Hamm

blabbing away
or someone buried in shit
who lost their house
in the wildfire
like being hit by lightning
or a virus
while dodging a bullet
or hitting a walk-off triple
in a bubble with nobody
in the stands
but cardboard cutouts
of people too sick
or scared
or locked down
to venture out
and they can't sleep
for the antibodies
and the bodies
they want
so they write
on tickertape hoping somebody
finds it in the street
after the parade
commemorating everyone
suffering at the same time
but differently
the way everyone makes love
differently and everyone's living
room is shockingly different
even in the same historic
senior housing they share
each asleep because the heat
is turned off at 10 and it gets too cold

to stay up
unless you're so hot
you can't stop
or you itch so much
you can't sleep
and you must find some way
to distract yourself
from scratching
how long can it last
you wonder
the pandemic the unending
catastrophes
when things were bad enough
before and now who knows
how lost they'll get
like a face mask
in the gutter
washed into the bay
with the first rain
and now it's too late
you've gone on too long
and you can't quit
because you're committed
and the band on your wrist
is inscribed in Chinese
like a fortune cookie
You will be showered with good luck

STEPHEN KESSLER is a California writer whose poetry and prose have appeared in hundreds of periodicals and dozens of books across the United States since the late 1960s. His translations from Spanish have received the Harold Morton Landon Translation Award from the Academy of American Poets, a Lambda Literary Award, the PEN Center USA Translation Award, a National Endowment for the Arts Fellowship, and a Northern California Book Award. As a journalist, essayist and critic he has written for numerous newspapers and magazines, mostly in Northern California. The literary newspaper he founded and edited for sixteen years (1999–2014), *The Redwood Coast Review,* was four times recipient of the PR Excellence Award of the California Library Association. He is the editor and principal translator of *The Sonnets* by Jorge Luis Borges and the author of three collections of essays and a novel, *The Mental Traveler.* Born in Los Angeles in 1947, he is a longtime resident of Santa Cruz and in recent years an op-ed columnist for the *Santa Cruz Sentinel.*

For more about Stephen Kessler, visit www.stephenkessler.com

BLACK WIDOW PRESS :: POETRY IN TRANSLATION

Approximate Man and Other Writings by Tristan Tzara. Translated and edited by Mary Ann Caws.

Art Poétique by Guillevic. Translated by Maureen Smith.

Beginnings of the Prose Poem. Edited by Mary Ann Caws, Michel Delville.

The Big Game by Benjamin Péret. Translated with an introduction by Marilyn Kallet.

Boris Vian Invents Boris Vian: A Boris Vian Reader. Edited and translated by Julia Older.

Capital of Pain by Paul Eluard. Translated by Mary Ann Caws, Patricia Terry, and Nancy Kline.

Chanson Dada: Selected Poems by Tristan Tzara. Translated with an introduction and essay by Lee Harwood.

Earthlight (Clair de Terre) by André Breton. Translated by Bill Zavatsky and Zack Rogow. (New and revised edition.)

Essential Poems and Prose of Jules Laforgue. Translated and edited by Patricia Terry.

Essential Poems and Writings of Joyce Mansour: A Bilingual Anthology. Translated with an introduction by Serge Gavronsky.

Essential Poems and Writings of Robert Desnos: A Bilingual Anthology. Edited with an introduction and essay by Mary Ann Caws.

EyeSeas (Les Ziaux) by Raymond Queneau. Translated with an introduction by Daniela Hurezanu and Stephen Kessler.

Fables in a Modern Key by Pierre Coran. Translated by Norman R. Shapiro. Full-color illustrations by Olga Pastuchiv.

Fables of Town & Country by Pierre Coran. Translated by Norman R. Shapiro. Full-color illustrations by Olga Pastuchiv.

A Flea the Size of Paris: The Old French Fatrasies & Fatras. Edited and translated by Ted Byrne and Donato Mancini.

Forbidden Pleasures: New Selected Poems 1924–1949 by Luis Cernuda. Translated by Stephen Kessler.

Furor and Mystery & Other Writings by René Char. Translated by Mary Ann Caws and Nancy Kline.

The Gentle Genius of Cécile Périn: Selected Poems (1906–1956). Edited and translated by Norman R. Shapiro.

The Great Madness by Avigdor Hameiri. Translated and edited by Peter C. Appelbaum with an introduction by Dan Hecht.

Guarding the Air: Selected Poems of Gunnar Harding. Translated and edited by Roger Greenwald.

Howls & Growls: French Poems to Bark By. Translated by Norman R. Shapiro; illustrated by Olga K. Pastuchiv.

I Have Invented Nothing: Selected Poems by Jean-Pierre Rosnay. Translated by J. Kates.

In Praise of Sleep: Selected Poems of Lucian Blaga. Translated with an introduction by Andrei Codrescu.

The Inventor of Love & Other Writings by Gherasim Luca. Translated by Julian & Laura Semilian. Introduction by Andrei Codrescu. Essay by Petre Răileanu.

Jules Supervielle: Selected Prose and Poetry. Translated by Nancy Kline & Patricia Terry.

La Fontaine's Bawdy by Jean de La Fontaine. Translated with an introduction by Norman R. Shapiro.

Last Love Poems of Paul Eluard. Translated with an introduction by Marilyn Kallet.

A Life of Poems, Poems of a Life by Anna de Noailles. Edited and translated by Norman R. Shapiro. Introduction by Catherine Perry.

Love, Poetry (L'amour la poésie) by Paul Eluard. Translated with an essay by Stuart Kendall.

Of Human Carnage—Odessa 1918–1920 by Avigdor Hameiri. Translated and edited by Peter C. Appelbaum with an introduction by Dan Hecht.

Pierre Reverdy: Poems, Early to Late. Translated by Mary Ann Caws and Patricia Terry.

Poems of André Breton: A Bilingual Anthology. Translated with essays by Jean-Pierre Cauvin and Mary Ann Caws.

Poems of A.O. Barnabooth by Valery Larbaud. Translated by Ron Padgett and Bill Zavatsky.

Poems of Consummation by Vicente Aleixandre. Translated by Stephen Kessler.

Préversities: A Jacques Prévert Sampler. Translated and edited by Norman R. Shapiro.

RhymAmusings (AmuseRimes) by Pierre Coran. Translated by Norman R. Shapiro.

The Sea and Other Poems by Guillevic. Translated by Patricia Terry. Introduction by Monique Chefdor.

Sixty Years: Selected Poems 1957–2017 by Mikhail Yeryomin. Translated by J. Kates. *(forthcoming)*

Through Naked Branches by Tarjei Vesaas. Translated, edited, and introduced by Roger Greenwald.

To Speak, to Tell You? Poems by Sabine Sicaud. Translated by Norman R. Shapiro. Introduction and notes by Odile Ayral-Clause.

BLACK WIDOW PRESS MODERN POETRY SERIES

WILLIS BARNSTONE
ABC of Translation
African Bestiary (forthcoming)

DAVE BRINKS
The Caveat Onus
The Secret Brain: Selected Poems 1995–2012

RUXANDRA CESEREANU
Crusader-Woman. Translated by Adam J. Sorkin. Introduction by Andrei Codrescu.
Forgiven Submarine by Ruxandra Cesereanu and Andrei Codrescu.

CLAYTON ESHLEMAN
An Alchemist with One Eye on Fire
Anticline
Archaic Design
Clayton Eshleman/The Essential Poetry: 1960–2015
Grindstone of Rapport: A Clayton Eshleman Reader
Penetralia
Pollen Aria
The Price of Experience
Endure: Poems by Bei Dao. Translated by Clayton Eshleman and Lucas Klein.
Curdled Skulls: Poems of Bernard Bador. Translated by Bernard Bador with Clayton Eshleman.

PIERRE JORIS
Barzakh (Poems 2000–2012)
Exile Is My Trade: A Habib Tengour Reader

MARILYN KALLET
How Our Bodies Learned
The Love That Moves Me
Packing Light: New and Selected Poems
Disenchanted City (La ville désenchantée) by Chantal Bizzini. Translated by J. Bradford Anderson, Darren Jackson, and Marilyn Kallet.

ROBERT KELLY
Fire Exit
The Hexagon

STEPHEN KESSLER
Garage Elegies
Last Call

BILL LAVENDER
Memory Wing

HELLER LEVINSON
from stone this running
LinguaQuake
Lurk
Seep
Tenebraed
Un-
Wrack Lariat

JOHN OLSON
Backscatter: New and Selected Poems
Dada Budapest
Larynx Galaxy
Weave of the Dream King

NIYI OSUNDARE
City Without People: The Katrina Poems

MEBANE ROBERTSON
An American Unconscious
Signal from Draco: New and Selected Poems

JEROME ROTHENBERG
Concealments and Caprichos
Eye of Witness: A Jerome Rothenberg Reader. Edited with commentaries by Heriberto Yepez & Jerome Rothenberg.
The President of Desolation & Other Poems

AMINA SAÏD.
The Present Tense of the World: Poems 2000–2009. Translated with an introduction by Marilyn Hacker.

ANIS SHIVANI
Soraya (Sonnets)

JERRY W. WARD, JR.
Fractal Song

BLACK WIDOW PRESS ANTHOLOGIES / BIOGRAPHIES

Barbaric Vast & Wild: A Gathering of Outside and Subterranean Poetry (*Poems for the Millennium,* vol. 5). Editors: Jerome Rothenberg and John Bloomberg-Rissman

Clayton Eshleman: The Whole Art by Stuart Kendall

Revolution of the Mind: The Life of André Breton by Mark Polizzotti